Portrait of a Decade

The 1980s

ELIZABETH CAMPLING

B.T. Batsford Ltd, London

Contents

The original idea for the Portrait of a Decade series was conceived by Trevor Fisher.

© Elizabeth Campling 1990
First published 1990

Typeset by Tek-Art Ltd Kent
and printed and bound
in Great Britain by
MacLehose and Partners Ltd, Portsmouth
for the publishers
B.T. Batsford Ltd
4 Fitzhardinge Street
London W1H 0AH

A CIP catalogue record for this book is available from the British Library

ISBN 0 7134 6209 4

Frontispiece: Pulling down the Iron Curtain: border guards using wire-cutters on the Hungarian-Austrian border, May 1989.

Introduction

The 1980s followed two decades of remarkable social and cultural experiment and change in the West, during which established beliefs in everything from politics to religion, sexual behaviour to the way children were educated were questioned. These two decades had also been an age of idealism. By the end of the 1970s, though, the dream had turned sour. Western confidence in her mission to save the world died in the jungles of Vietnam. The great recession and oil crisis of 1974-5 and the inflation that followed dented the West's faith in her economic future. Widespread violence and terrorism made the world seem a frightening place to many people. The climax came, perhaps, in 1979, when the American embassy in Teheran was taken over by Islamic revolutionaries and its staff held hostage, while the mighty USA looked on helplessly. Britain, on the other hand, seemed to be sinking into economic decline and chaos. The 1980s, in many ways, were a reaction against all this.

The new conservatism

By 1980 it was clear that many of the changes in social and sexual behaviour had come to stay, so too had some of the advances made by women and ethnic groups. In other areas, though, from education to economics, the values of the 1960s and 1970s were under fire. Most marked was the growing belief everywhere that a person's first duty was not to society as a whole but to their own welfare and that of the family, and that too much collective action did not wipe out hardship but made people lazy and unenterprising. More and more people, for example, were reluctant to pay high taxes to finance social services or keep workers in employment. Those who thought this way believed they were just turning the clock back to values of an earlier and better age, when people were more self-reliant. 'Victorian values', they were labelled by Britain's Mrs Thatcher. At the same time, the break with the past two decades was so deep that it was almost a revolution in itself. Two politicians above all, who were to dominate the 1980s in the West, spearheaded this conservative revolution – Ronald Reagan, President of the USA from 1980 to 1988, and Margaret Thatcher, Prime Minister of Britain from 1979. Whether they created the new mood, as their enemies claimed, or were themselves only swept along by what was happening anyway at the grassroots, no one really knew. Perhaps it was a bit of both.

Mrs Thatcher, the British Prime Minister, waving to crowds on her victory in 1979 that was to pave the way for the domination of 'conservative values' in the 1980s.

The conservative revolution triumphs

By the middle of the decade, the mood of most Western societies was changing fast. Out had gone what Mrs Thatcher dubbed the 'Nanny state', which looked after the welfare of its citizens and protected them against hardship. In had come the 'enterprise culture' and the cult of self-reliance. Making money and spending it became respectable again. The role-models of the age were the successful self-made men like Richard Branson of Virgin Records or Alan Sugar of Amstrad computers. The enterprise culture even gave the English language a new word – 'yuppie'. Terms like 'market forces'

Introduction

and 'cost-effectiveness' became a familiar part of the everyday language, even among those who did not approve of the way things were going. After a wobbly start, the Western economies recovered and boomed. By mid-decade most people were doing well, but some – those who were too old, too unskilled or who lived in the wrong parts of the country – were left behind, leaving pockets of deprivation in the midst of affluent societies. It was a far cry from the 1960s dream of social equality.

The revival of the West

With economic recovery the West's faith in itself was reborn. Nowhere was this better shown than in the self-confidence of Reagan and Thatcher on the world stage. Reagan took up again the old crusade for 'American values' – against Libya and the Soviet Union, in Central America and Grenada. Thatcher's Britain fought and won a war against Argentina.

More revolutions

The West was not the only place to have a social revolution that left its mark on the 1980s. After decades of exploitation at the hands of developed nations, the Islamic world was borne along on a resurgence of pride and consciousness, heavily tinged with bitterness, especially towards the USA. It had begun in Iran in 1979 and was to play a key role in world politics and to pose problems for societies everywhere – from Britain to the USSR – who had Muslims among their citizens.

After years of stagnation, great changes swept the USSR after Mr Gorbachev came to power in 1985. Under the slogans of perestroika and glasnost – words that became as familiar to non-Russians as most words in their own language – he set out to reform Soviet society as it had not been reformed since the 1917 Revolution. The result was a more open and humane society but a more violent and unstable one too, as long-supressed nationalist and racial tensions surfaced, and promises of rapid economic improvement failed to materialize. At the close of the 1980s the USSR was in deep crisis.

The end of an era?

The most dramatic events of the 1980s waited until the very end. Since 1945 the Cold War had been a fact of life for both East and West, and at the beginning of the 1980s nuclear war seemed as likely as it had ever done. With the arrival of Gorbachev, all this began to change, and by 1989 a real end to the arms race and superpower rivalry seemed in sight. And in a wave of revolutions, peaceful for the most part, Eastern Europe, for so long under the thumb of Soviet might, was allowed to break free, and the Iron Curtain was torn down. This spelt danger as well as hope, for dreams of freedom and prosperity could all too easily decay into frustration and violence, as was already happening in the USSR itself. When the decade ended, though, hopes for world peace were higher than at any time since 1945. It was even

Iranian women join the mobilization parade as part of the Ayatollah's jihad.

Introduction

possible that future generations might see the 1980s as one of history's great turning points.

The future under threat

Genetic engineering was the great scientific breakthrough of the 1980s, although it gave rise to grave moral dilemmas. The microchip revolution continued to work its way into daily life, at home and at work, in hundreds of different ways. The fear, first voiced in the 1970s, that modern technology was damaging the world around us went on mounting as scientists discovered that the very atmosphere itself was under threat. Terms like the 'greenhouse effect' and 'ozone layer' came into the everyday vocabulary. And a new killer disease, AIDS, struck fear into millions and forced people to change the way they ran their sex lives. By the end of the decade the permissive society was on the way out, while AIDS and the environment were at the forefront of public concern.

The culture of materialism

In the 1980s commercial pressures came to play an even larger part in sport and the arts. As government subsidies dropped off, it became more important than ever for a play or record to appeal to a mass audience or attract a private sponsor. Either way, quality or originality were often sacrificed for instant appeal. Records were sold on the strength of the glossy videos that accompanied them, and classy musicals like *Cats* or *Starlight Express* found it easier to get put on than less commercial plays.

At the same time, there *were* examples of original culture around, such as black American hip-hop music, and not all artists were interested only in making money. Inspired by Bob Geldof, pop stars staged spectacular fund raisers for famine relief in Africa, and a number of musicians involved themselves in political causes as well. Live Aid, Sports Aid and Comic Relief were supported by huge audiences and they all raised millions of pounds for the poor – both at home and abroad.

A decade to love or hate

By the end of the 1980s, opinion in the West – still riding high on an economic boom, which had slowed down a bit since the mid-decade – was divided over all that had happened. To some, the woolly idealism of the 1960s and 1970s had given way to a healthy spirit of realism, which accepted that humans were basically selfish and acquisitive and built on that. Others found the new society greedy and uncaring, only too ready to throw its weaker members to the wall. Some of the decade's great changes like the Islamic revival and the liberalization of the USSR and break-up of its empire in Eastern Europe were still going on and no one could see where or how they would end. And now in the forefront of human concern was the future of the poisoned environment of planet Earth itself.

Signs of exhaustion show on the face of Live Aid organizer, Bob Geldof, after the culmination of months of hard work to raise money for the famine victims of Ethiopia.

1980

Polish

The monolith

SINCE THE 1940S the Soviet Union had held Eastern Europe in a firm grip. No alternative political parties that might challenge the hold of the Communist Party had ever been allowed to take root, nor rival opinions tolerated. The Brezhnev Doctrine of 1968 had asserted the right of the Soviet Union to intervene, by force if necessary, in any country where a Communist government looked likely to collapse.

Lech Walesa, the leader of the first independent Polish trade union, Solidarity.

Polish government in trouble

BY 1980, THOUGH, the Communist rulers of Poland were in deep trouble. The country had a debt of over $24,000 million. In June, Party Secretary Gierek announced huge increases in the prices of all essential goods from electricity to meat. Poles, whose standard of living was already one of the lowest in Europe, faced, he confessed, 'five austere years'. Like a volcano that has long been quietly smouldering, the country erupted.

The workers revolt

A RASH OF PROTEST STRIKES broke out all over the country. By August over 150 major factories were idle, so too were the 200,000 miners of Silesia. The Catholic Church, to which – despite three decades of anti-religious propaganda – most Poles still belonged, publicly criticized the Communist leadership for economic mismanagement. Students and intellectuals spoke out. On 14 August the giant Lenin shipyard at Gdańsk on the Baltic came out, under the leadership of a 38-year-old electrician, Lech Walesa, who had been sacked twice before for illegal political activities. Three days later the Gdańsk strikers issued a list of their demands, which were soon taken up by all the other striking factories, including the right to form independent trade unions, the right to strike and the release of political prisoners. The Polish Communist Party, it was now clear, was facing something much bigger than just an outburst of ordinary strikes.

Workers Revolt

First round to the strikers

ON 30 AUGUST the government, faced with turmoil, gave in and conceded most of the strikers' demands. The strikes were called off. For the Polish Communist Party it was a defeat of a kind that had never happened before in the Soviet bloc. It was also a slap in the face for the Russians, for the Poles were rebelling against years of domination by their powerful eastern neighbour. Religious symbolism became a gesture of defiance. Whenever Walesa spoke, he hung a crucifix above his head. 'These are not only a symbol of devotion', explained a colleague, 'they symbolize Poland reborn, the Poland of the movement.'

We are now co-masters of this land.
Lech Walesa to Gdańsk shipyard workers as they voted to call the strike off, 1 September

The situation is fast developing into one of the greatest challenges to a Communist regime yet. When you start talking about free trade unions, then you are undermining the whole Communist system . . . . The myth

Free trade union born

SIX DAYS after the Gdańsk agreement, Gierek resigned. The official reason given was ill-health, but to many Poles it was a sign that the once all-powerful Party had lost its nerve. Their confidence surged. With the easing of censorship the newspapers and television were opened to a flood of free speech such as Poland had not known since the war. On 22 September the first independent trade union, legalized by the agreement of 30 August, was launched. Called *Solidarnosc* or 'Solidarity', it was open to all workers. Within weeks, eight million had joined. Its leader was Lech Walesa, now a folk hero, whose face was more familiar to Poles and foreigners alike than any Party leader's had ever been.

of the workers' dictatorship is becoming a reality.
Western diplomat in Warsaw, August 1980, quoted in *Time* magazine, 25 August

Euphoria – and fear

BY THE END of the year few in Poland doubted that the people had won a historic victory. But while euphoria ran high, so too did grave fears for the future. The upheavals of the autumn had further damaged the limping economy, creating serious shortages of almost everything. For many people the political excitement was outweighed by the grim daily struggle to keep going. Above all, though, hung the spectre of Poland's mighty neighbour. So far the Soviet Union had held her hand, but when, or if, the patience of Brezhnev, the Soviet leader, would finally run out no one knew, but the closing weeks of 1980 brought ominous signs. Soviet divisions massed on the frontier and Moscow issued veiled warnings reminiscent of the ones that had been thrown at Czechoslovakia in 1968 before the takeover there. At the turn of the year Poland was balanced on a knife-edge.

REMEMBER THE CZECHS
Moscow, 30 November
The Soviet Union issued an implicit warning today that the Soviet bloc states could take action in Poland on the line of the 1968 intervention in Czechoslovakia to save Polish communism from 'counter-revolution'.

The warning came in a newspaper article in Prague's *Rude Pravo*, comparing the 'crisis situation' in Poland with that in Czechoslovakia 12 years ago.
The Times, 1 December

Solidarity wins the next round

ON 24 OCTOBER a Warsaw court registered Solidarity as a legal organization but insisted on inserting a clause in the union's constitution recognizing the 'leading role' of the Party in the life of the nation. Walesa threatened to bring the country out on strike again, and few doubted that he could do it if he chose. Once again the authorities gave in. The offending clause was withdrawn and Solidarity won the right to free access to all the mass media. For the first time a ruling Communist Party had been forced to share power and listen to the uncensored voices of the people it was supposed to represent. One of Solidarity's first demands was a memorial to the workers killed by security forces during riots in Gdańsk in 1970. Over 100,000 people attended its consecration in December.

A Superpower humiliated

THE HUMILIATION of the mighty United States of America by the Islamic Republic of Iran went on. In April President Carter's patience snapped and he authorized 'Operation Eagle's Claw', a daring rescue by helicopter. It ended in fiasco and disaster when, 200 miles from their target, mechanical failures forced the helicopters to turn back. On the way home two of them collided, leaving eight men dead. Carter, who had faced fierce criticism for his failure to free the hostages earlier, was now despised for his inability to pull off the rescue attempt. At the end of the year, the 55 hostages still had not been released – after 423 days in captivity.

Islam on the march

THE MOOD IN IRAN threatened to destabilize the whole region. In February a call went out from Ayatollah Khomeini for a *jihad* or holy war to spread the Islamic revolution into neighbouring states like Iraq and Saudi Arabia. The West was disturbed as well, for the Persian Gulf region was crucial to their oil supplies. President Carter suspected that the USSR might take advantage of the chaos to establish a foothold in the region and make the Gulf yet another Cold War battle-ground. In fact, the Russians, with 50 million Muslims of their own, feared the upsurge of Islamic militancy as much as anyone. The tensions even came to London in April, when anti-Khomeini gunmen seized the Iranian Embassy and held 20 people hostage. The siege ended a week later only after a spectacular raid by the élite Special Air Services (SAS). The Embassy building was left a burnt-out shell.

An attempt by any outside force to gain control of the Persian Gulf region will be regarded as an assault on the vital interests of the United States. It will be repelled by any means necessary, including military force.
From Carter's 'State of the Union' message to Congress, 30 January, which became known as the 'Carter Doctrine'.

The Middle East.

Russia meets her Vietnam

THE SOVIET INVASION of Afghanistan on Christmas Eve 1979 had been intended as a short, sharp action to prop up the tottering Communist regime there. The result was the opposite, for it produced such a backlash among the fiercely proud Muslim people that thousands took to the hills to form anti-Communist guerilla bands – the Mujaheddin. Like the Americans in Vietnam before them, the Red Army soon discovered just how difficult it was to find and destroy fanatical guerillas in rugged terrain. Although more and more Russian troops poured in, they could not bring the countryside under control. By the end of the year, a quick withdrawal seemed as far away as ever.

War in the Gulf

THE SIMMERING HOSTILITY between Iran and Iraq erupted into full-scale war in September. Within weeks a 10 mile strip of Iranian territory along the border, including the big oil refineries at Abadan and Kharg Island and the port of Korramshahr, were in Iraqi hands. Over a million Iranian refugees had fled the region. The war spread further alarm in the West for the safety of her oil supplies coming through the Gulf. There were few signs, though, that the fighting would be over quickly, for the Iraqi advance had ground to a halt by the end of the year, and the two sides were locked into a bloody stalemate.

Cold War hots up

THE INVASION of Afghanistan soured relations between the Superpowers. President Carter swore that the Soviet Union would be made to pay for her aggression. SALT II was put on ice and the sale of surplus US grain cancelled. In July American athletes boycotted the Moscow Olympics. Defence spending went up. The Polish situation heightened the tension. By the end of 1980 relations between East and West were more fraught than they had been for many a year.

Third World crippled by debt

THE STEEP RISE in oil prices caused another economic recession in the West but that was nothing compared to the plight of many Third World countries. A report by a panel of international experts known as the Brandt Report tried to draw the world's attention to this. As well as hunger and poverty, many African and South American nations – the 'South' – were staggering under a crippling burden of debt to Western banks. For some countries, just the interest on the debts came to almost as much as their whole annual budget. The problem was now so serious that it threatened the future well-being of the whole planet. Only by creating a more just global economic system, even if that meant sacrifices on the part of the more prosperous developed world (which Brandt called the 'North'), could catastrophe be avoided.

Prime Minister Robert Mugabe makes his address at Zimbabwe's independence ceremony.

America elects an actor as President

IN THE PRESIDENTIAL elections on 4 November, Americans overwhelmingly rejected the unlucky President Carter and chose in his place a former movie actor, Ronald Reagan, who promised a return to the traditional values of self-reliance and religion and to restore America's self-confidence and pride at home and abroad. Carter won only six out of the 50 states.

Zimbabwe: a new nation

AT MIDNIGHT ON 18 APRIL white-ruled Rhodesia became the independent African state of Zimbabwe, with Robert Mugabe as its first black Prime Minister. Whether the new nation could overcome its hard legacy of racial and tribal conflict remained to be seen. Mugabe urged whites to stay and promised to be fair. The time for hate was past, he told the crowd gathered for the independence ceremonies.

Dissident silenced

IN A NEW WAVE of repression against dissidents, the Soviet Union's most famous critic, physicist Andrei Sakharov, was exiled with his wife to the closed city of Gorky, where he could no longer meet foreigners or publicize his views.

Mrs Thatcher sticks to her guns

FACED WITH BRITAIN'S worst recession since the 1930s, Conservative Prime Minister Margaret Thatcher stuck to her course. Britain's economic troubles, she believed, were not just the result of short-term crises like rising oil prices but symptomatic of a much deeper malaise, which included chronic wage inflation, inefficient and overmanned industry, overpowerful unions and too much government expenditure in areas where people should be looking after themselves. The answer lay in stringent spending cuts and a ruthless streamlining of inefficient industries, even if that meant rising unemployment and hardship for some. One of her first targets was the unprofitable steel industry, where widespread closures and redundancies led to the first national steel strike since 1926. It lasted three months. By the autumn unemployment was over two million and the government was becoming very unpopular, but at the Tory Party conference Mrs Thatcher told wavering party members that there was no turning back.

This country is going through the rough but necessary ride of the patient, who for a time is suffering from both the illness and the medicine . . . There are no soft answers . . . This lady's not for turning.
From Mrs Thatcher's speech to the Conservative Party conference, 10 October

Music reflects a troubled society

THE POPULAR MUSIC of 1980 reflected the troubled society around it. In Britain the punk tradition of disillusion and rebellion was carried on by groups like The Clash, The Gang of Four, Raincoats and Red Crayola. So too was the cult among white groups like The Specials and The Police for West Indian Ska and bluebeat music. In complete contrast were the New Romantics – groups like Spandau Ballet, Visage, Depeche Mode, Ultravox and Duran Duran. Rejecting the images of the punk era, they went in for exotic and colourful clothes and grew their hair long. Their music, which relied heavily on clever electronic effects, did not carry a message but was meant for dancing to.

Some films of 1980
Nine to Five, a feminist comedy, starring Jane Fonda, Lily Tomlin and Dolly Parton.
The Long Good Friday, starring Bob Hoskins, which became a gangster classic.
The Tin Drum, based on the novel by Günter Grass: an unusual view of the rise of Nazism.
The Elephant Man
Heaven's Gate, a three-and-a-half hour epic by the maker of *The Deer Hunter* (1978), which was a commercial flop.

Borg wins Wimbledon again

BJORN BORG OF SWEDEN won the Wimbledon men's singles title for a record fifth time when he beat the up-and-coming American, John McEnroe.

My ambition is to be remembered as the greatest player of all time. I guess you could say I have come close.
Bjorn Borg after his Wimbledon win, 5 July

The larger-than-life characters Pam and Bobby Ewing, stars of Dallas.

Escapist films popular

THE SAME URGE for escapism was seen in the cinema. There were some interesting films in circulation, including a number of low-budget British films about the alienation of youth like *Rude Boy, Babylon* and *Breaking Glass*. None of these attracted as much attention, though, as the American space blockbuster *The Empire Strikes Back*, the sequel to *Star Wars*, which was the commercial hit of the year in the USA and Britain. And even that could not match the worldwide popularity of the US TV series *Dallas*, the saga of a rich Texan family, the Ewings. It had an estimated 300 million viewers in 55 countries, 22 million of them in Britain. In its luxurious lifestyle and its larger-than-life passions and grudges, *Dallas* was the ultimate in escapist entertainment.

It opened the way for a flood of American soap operas on all three televison channels.

John Lennon shot dead

FORMER BEATLE John Lennon, perhaps the most famous and influential musician of the 1960s, was shot and killed outside his apartment in New York on 8 December.

Moscow Olympics go ahead without the Americans

THE AMERICAN boycott meant that some of the world's top athletes did not compete in the 1980 Olympics, and few world records were broken. The most gripping event was the clash between the world's two best middle-distance runners, Sebastian Coe and Steve Ovett of Britain. In the 800 m Ovett beat Coe into second place, but Coe won the 1500 m the next day. Daley Thompson became the first Briton ever to win the decathlon. As usual, East Germans dominated male and female swimming.

English club triumphs in Europe again

FOR THE SECOND YEAR running, Nottingham Forest won the European Cup, beating Hamburg SV 1-0. British club sides now had an outstanding record in European competitions, but the national side slumped again. They were knocked out of the European championship before the semi-finals. Before the match with Italy, drunken English fans went on the rampage in Turin. The games themselves produced mostly the dull, defensive kind of football that had become fashionable in the 1970s.

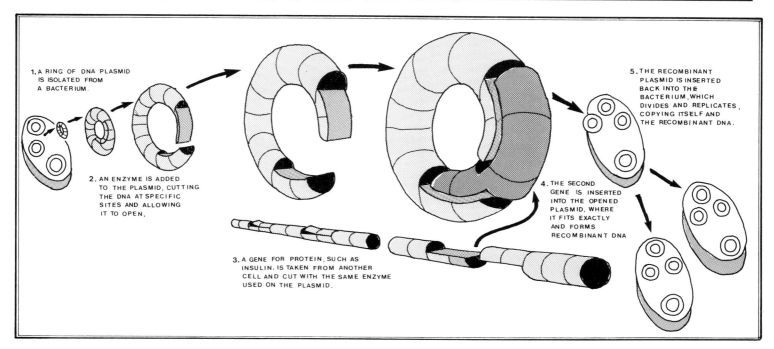

1. A RING OF DNA PLASMID IS ISOLATED FROM A BACTERIUM.

2. AN ENZYME IS ADDED TO THE PLASMID, CUTTING THE DNA AT SPECIFIC SITES AND ALLOWING IT TO OPEN.

3. A GENE FOR PROTEIN, SUCH AS INSULIN, IS TAKEN FROM ANOTHER CELL AND CUT WITH THE SAME ENZYME USED ON THE PLASMID.

4. THE SECOND GENE IS INSERTED INTO THE OPENED PLASMID, WHERE IT FITS EXACTLY AND FORMS RECOMBINANT DNA.

5. THE RECOMBINANT PLASMID IS INSERTED BACK INTO THE BACTERIUM, WHICH DIVIDES AND REPLICATES, COPYING ITSELF AND THE RECOMBINANT DNA.

Breakthrough in genetic engineering

How genetic engineering works.

FOR THE FIRST TIME scientists in Britain and the USA successfully took genes from the DNA of one organism and transplanted them into another, when the gene that made insulin in humans was planted into bacteria. When the bacteria reproduced themselves, the insulin-making gene was reproduced as well. This process was known as genetic engineering. Its future possibilities were endless. Common bacteria could be turned into living factories turning out vast quantities of vital medical substances, including vaccines, antibodies and hormones like insulin. Diseases caused by genetic defects might be cured by inserting the correct version of the defective gene into the human body, although a first attempt to treat two thalassaemia (a hereditary form of severe anaemia) patients in this way failed. Companies like Celltech in the USA were set up to exploit the new technology. Among its first plans was a plant to make insulin. For all its possible benefits, genetic engineering worried many people. Once man started interfering with nature in this way, there was no knowing where it might end. Unscrupulous scientists might even use genetic engineering to create a new super-race.

Saturn data mystify scientists

ONCE AGAIN it was brought home how little man, for all his technological achievements, understood the mysteries of the universe. In September the American *Voyager 1*, after a 38-month journey, flew within 70,000 miles of the planet Saturn and sent back the clearest pictures yet. Although scientists now had far more data to work with, much of it was puzzling. Three new moons were discovered. Parts of the famous rings of Saturn were now seen as separate structures plaited together like pieces of rope; not an easy phenomenon to explain.

World's wildlife in danger

GROWING FEARS about the environment were confirmed by the publication of a United Nations report in March. Between half a million and one million species of plants and animals would soon be extinct because of the activities of man. Every year, for example, saw the destruction of an area of tropical rainforest the size of Wales. Not only would many vital sources of food and medicine disappear but the very future of the planet would be endangered. Fewer trees meant more carbon dioxide in the atmosphere, which might alter the climate. Rainwater tended to run off the land faster, stripping the topsoil off and causing drought in some areas and flooding in others. If nothing was done by the year 2000, the damage would be beyond repair.

1981 Recession Hits

Gloomy prospects

1980 HAD SEEN THE START of another recession in the West. Factory closures and unemployment rose sharply everywhere. Inflation was high. In most countries public expenditure on everything from defence to social security far outstripped income, leading to a massive burden of public debt or budget deficit. Nowhere was the problem worse than in the United States, where the outgoing Carter administration announced in January that it was leaving its successor an estimated debt of $56 billion. For nations that had been geared for decades to the idea that productivity and living standards would go on rising for ever these were worrying times. The prognosis for 1981 was gloomy indeed.

Industrial production in the world's leading economies.

Reaganomics hits USA

IN THE USA PRESIDENT REAGAN brought in high interest rates and sweeping cuts in public expenditure, slashing welfare programmes that helped the unemployed, low-paid and one-parent families. Cuts of up to 25 per cent in personal taxes were scheduled over the next 33 months. His aims were moral as well as economic, for he believed that too much government was an evil and that self-reliance would strengthen the moral fibre of the nation. The immediate effect of 'Reaganomics', as it was dubbed by the press, was a deepening of the recession. By the autumn nine million were out of work – almost 9 per cent of the population of working age – but inflation had dropped. Most heavily hit were automobile and steel production, turning whole areas like Youngstown, Ohio, and parts of Detroit and Pittsburgh into ghost towns. The dollar remained weak. The burden of monetarism fell most heavily on the poor but millions of ordinary Americans, neither poor nor unemployed, were also stunned by the effect of high interest rates on their standard of living.

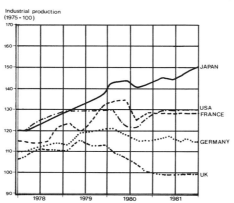

Industrial production
(1975 = 100)

JAPAN

USA
FRANCE

GERMANY

UK

For many consumers the high interest rates are quickly destroying the American dream of an ever increasing standard of living, including bigger homes, flashier cars and newer gadgets. Nowhere is this more evident than in the housing market. Just a decade ago, many Americans expected to own their own homes; today fewer do . . . the reason: sky high mortgage rates. The construction industry jokes that it now takes two working wives to afford a house.
Time, 19 July 1981

Economists prescribe harsh cure

THE SOLUTIONS put forward by most economists were uncomfortable ones. To some like Milton Friedman inflation was the main evil and must be tackled first by restricting the amount of money in circulation through wage freezes, high interest rates and cuts in public expenditure, even though this would deepen the recession in the short term. This idea became known as 'Monetarism'. Moreover, the recession was not a temporary hiccup or a fluke but due to the long-term mismanagement of Western industries, especially the traditional heavy ones like steel, cars, shipbuilding or heavy engineering, which were overmanned and paid their workers too much. The answer was to streamline industry, even if this meant replacing men by sophisticated machinery and closing unprofitable factories. Tax-cuts, especially for the well-off, would encourage enterprise and hard work and thus stimulate the economy as a whole. In the short term many would suffer, but in the long-term a revitalized industrial base would bring new jobs and prosperity would trickle down to everyone. This was the 'enterprise culture'.

The People's March for Jobs, from Liverpool to London, evokes memories of scenes during the Great Depression of the 1930s.

the West

No U-turn for Mrs Thatcher

BRITAIN HAD BEEN FOLLOWING its own form of monetarism since 1979. The press nicknamed it 'Thatcherism'. By the autumn unemployment had hit a total of three million, a level not reached since the Great Depression of the 1930s. The suffering was not evenly spread. Unemployment was highest in the old industrial heartland of Scotland, South Wales and the North of England and among ethnic minorities and the young. The South was affected far less. By the end of 1981 one in seven of the under-25 age group had been out of work for over six months. Mrs Thatcher, though, remained adamant that her programme would work in the long run. In the autumn she ousted the doubters – whom the press dubbed 'Wets' – from her cabinet and replaced

them with men after her own heart, including Norman Tebbit, who earned notoriety when he criticized those who demonstrated against unemployment: 'My father (who was out of work in the 1930s) did not riot', he told delegates at the Conservative Party conference in September. 'He got on his bike and looked for work.'

Europe in trouble

THE REST OF EUROPE did not escape, bringing fears of social upheaval. Even in West Germany, whose booming economy had once been held up as a model to the rest of the world, unemployment was reaching the one-and-a-half million mark by the close of the year.

We run the danger in the West of running an economy, one of the by-products of which is the pauperization of large sections of our community. This is bound to put immense strains on the social fabric of our societies . . . I expect to see an alarming rise in alcoholism, crime, extremist politics and street violence. I would not be surprised to see terrorism rise again.

Ivor Richard, the EEC's Commissioner for Social Policy, in an interview in *Time* magazine, 12 October 1981

Nations urged to get together

IN OCTOBER DELEGATES from 22 nations met at Caucun in Mexico to discuss the world economic crisis. High on the agenda was the Brandt Report. There were few signs, though, that the people of the West would forget their own troubles long enough to take notice of Brandt's plea that North and South should work together to end the crisis.

. . . the world economy is now functioning so badly that it damages both the immediate and longer-run interests of all nations. The problems of poverty and hunger are becoming more serious . . . fast-growing population, with another two billion people in the next two decades, will cause much greater strains on the world's food and resources. The industrial capacity of the North is under-used, causing unemployment . . . while the South is in urgent need of the goods that the North could produce . . . real solutions can only be found if all nations work together towards a global solution.

North-South: A Programme for Survival, by the Independent Commission on International Developmental Issues, published 1980.

Hostages released

ON 21 JANUARY, HALF-AN-HOUR after Ronald Reagan had been sworn in as President of the USA, the 55 American hostages held in Teheran were finally released after 444-days. The timing was deliberate – a slap in the face for Carter. The news was received with rejoicing all over the United States, but memory of the long humiliation lived on. Reagan swore that any future repetition of such violence against Americans abroad would bring 'swift and effective retribution'. This warlike language went down well with his countrymen.

Martial Law declared in Poland

THE SITUATION IN POLAND staggered from crisis to crisis throughout the year. Solidarity, now ten million strong, demanded further big changes, including free elections. Daily strikes and demonstrations went on. The economy deteriorated rapidly, bringing severe shortages. On 9 February an army general, Jaruzelski, became Prime Minister. On the 5 December the Soviet Union accused the Poles of indulging in an 'anti-Soviet and anti-socialist orgy.' Ten days later General Jaruzelski declared martial law and the army took over. All strikes and demonstrations were banned and communications with the rest of the world cut. Over 40,000 people, including over 70 per cent of the Solidarity leadership, were interned. Walesa himself was put under house arrest and became the world's most famous political prisoner. The USSR denied any involvement in what had happened, but most observers saw the hand of the Russians behind Jaruzelski.

Thank goodness it's over! After the formal ceremony at St Paul's, the first chance to relax for the Prince and Princess of Wales, their bridesmaids and page boys.

Islamic revival spreads

ISLAMIC HOSTILITY TOWARDS the West spread out far beyond Iran. One of the bitterest enemies was Colonel Gadaffi of Libya, who was rumoured to be behind many of the acts of terrorism carried out on Americans abroad. Tensions boiled over in August when US and Libyan military jets clashed over the Gulf of Sidra off the Libyan coast. Two Libyan aircraft were shot down. Another spin-off from the growth of Islamic militancy occurred in October, when President Sadat of Egypt, who was seen by many Muslims as a traitor because of his reconciliation with Israel, was assassinated by members of an extremist Muslim sect. He was succeeded by Vice-President Mubarak.

Reagan declares a new Cold War

IN JANUARY, Reagan's new Secretary of State, General Haig, denounced the USSR in forthright terms. Their aim was no less than world domination and it was they who were behind most of the left-wing revolutions that took place in the Third World and many acts of terrorism. The time had now come for the West to make a firm stand, whatever the risk. Plans were drawn up for the largest military build-up in US history. American weapons systems in Europe were to be updated with the latest Cruise and Pershing 2 medium-range nuclear missiles. Reagan's views were shared by Britain's Prime Minister, Mrs Thatcher. The Russians dubbed her the 'Iron Lady'.

Wedding of the Year

IN A GLITTERING SPECTACLE that was in sharp contrast to the economic gloom all around, the Prince of Wales, heir to the British throne, married Lady Diana Spencer in St Paul's Cathedral on 29 July. Over 700 million viewers all over the world watched the event on television.

Britain's cities erupt

IN THE SPRING and summer of 1981 rioting came to the streets of Britain. It began in Brixton in south London in April. Then for a week in July many cities, including London, Wolverhampton, Birmingham, and the Toxteth area of Liverpool were torn apart by nights of violence. Gangs of youths – black and white – rampaged

Youths attack vehicles and police in Brixton during a summer of rioting.

the streets. Over 250 were injured. Theories as to why it had happened varied. Some blamed the recession, which had hit the inner-cities and the black community particularly hard. A commission under Lord Scarman was set up to investigate the causes. The Scarman Report when it came out in November laid most of the blame on years of 'racial disadvantage' and the consequent breakdown of trust in the authorities.

IRA hunger-strikers die

IN MARCH IRA PRISONERS in the Maze Prison in Belfast began a hunger strike in protest against the British government's refusal to give them special status as political prisoners. Seven weeks later the first of them, Bobby Sands, died, and the tension that was always close to the surface in Northern Ireland rose to boiling point. Eight days of rioting in Catholic areas of Belfast followed. Before the hunger strikes were called off in October, nine more prisoners had died. The IRA took their revenge by planting a bomb outside Chelsea Barracks in London, injuring 40 soldiers and killing two passers-by.

British politics in ferment

IN BRITAIN the Labour Party, rent by deep divisions of its own, was unable to take advantage of the unpopularity of Mrs Thatcher's government. Since 1979 the influence of the left-wing had been growing. In May, local elections put some big city councils including Liverpool and the Greater London Council (GLC) in the hands of left-wingers like Derek Hatton and Ken Livingstone. The press dubbed them the 'loony left'. Four former Labour ministers, Shirley Williams, Roy Jenkins, David Owen and William

Rodgers (the so-called 'Gang of Four') who disliked the way the Party was going, broke away to form an alternative, middle-of-the-road Social Democratic Party (SDP). In June they formed an electoral alliance with the tiny Liberal Party. In July the new alliance won two dramatic by-election victories – at Warrington and Croydon. It seemed as if the two-party mould that had dominated British politics for so long might be breaking, and the future seemed wide open.

Women protest against Cruise

IN DECEMBER WOMEN set up a camp outside the American air force base at Greenham Common in Berkshire, where Cruise missiles were due to arrive in 1983. In spite of attempts by the police to evict them for trespassing, they swore they would do everything they could to prevent the installation of the missiles.

Pop videos become the rage

ON 1 AUGUST THE MTV cable station, which broadcast nothing but pop videos for 12 hours a day, opened in the USA. MTV did not pay for the videos it showed but gave artists what amounted to free advertising time. Overnight any new release that wanted to make it to the top came out with its own video. This helped to make the New Romantics, who were attractive to look at, the most popular and commercially successful groups of 1981. One of the best examples of this was Duran Duran, whose slick video for *Girls on Film* catapaulted them to fame in Britain and the USA.

Top Sounds of 1981

Singles
Don't You Want Me – Human League
Vienna – Ultravox
Ghost Town – The Specials
Prince Charming – Adam and the Ants

Albums
Duran Duran – Duran Duran
Dare – Human League

Religious revival hits USA

OVER THE PAST FEW YEARS fundamentalist or evangelical Christianity had been spreading in the USA. Fundamentalists took the teachings of the Bible, including the Old Testament, word for word and had a strict moral code that rejected the permissive society of the 1960s and 1970s. A campaign was launched to clean up television. It organized a boycott of products made by firms who sponsored 'immoral' programmes like *Dallas*, *Charlies Angels* and *The Dating Game*. Television preachers like the Revd Jerry Falwell attracted an audience of millions.

London stages its first Marathon

THE 1970S HEALTH CRAZE was not over. Over 17,000 ran in this year's New York marathon. London staged its first-ever marathon on 29 March. It attracted nearly 7000 runners.

Sporting Highlights

- Borg's great winning run at Wimbledon was broken by 22-year-old John McEnroe, who beat him in the final.

- In a remarkable ten days in August Coe and Ovett broke the world 1500 m record three times between them.

Ovett and Coe battling it out in the 1500 metres.

British films win acclaim

COMPARATIVELY FEW British films were made in 1981 but two that were won widespread praise. They were *Chariots of Fire*, directed by David Puttnam, and *The French Lieutenant's Woman*, starring Meryl Streep and Jeremy Irons. The stream of films out of Australia continued, including *Breaker Morant*, which earned good reviews, and *Gallipoli*, which was a commercial and critical flop. Andrzej Wajda from Poland made *Man of Iron* about the birth of Solidarity. The US went on bringing out the blockbusters, including *Superman II*, which was a hit at the box office, and Warren Beatty's *Reds*, which was not. A realistic American TV police series, *Hill Street Blues*, won many awards.

England win an astounding victory

PERHAPS THE MOST REMARKABLE story of the year was that of cricketer Ian Botham. Since he had been appointed England captain in 1980, his play had slumped and so had England's. Against the Australians that summer, it was the same story. England lost one test match and drew the other. Botham gave up the captaincy. The third test looked set to become yet another disaster, when England had to follow on. Bookmakers' odds against them winning were 500-1. Then Botham came on, a new man. From 149 balls he scored 148 runs, forcing Australia to bat again. When they did, they were destroyed by the bowling of Bob Willis, who took eight wickets for 43 runs. England won. It was the most remarkable turn around in the history of modern cricket. Botham put in outstanding performances in the fourth and fifth tests too. Against all the odds, England won the Ashes.

Shuttle goes up – and comes down again

THE AMERICAN SPACE SHUTTLE *Columbia*, the world's first reusable spacecraft, took off on her maiden voyage on 11 April. After 36 orbits and 54 hours it flew back down through the earth's atmosphere and landed in the Mojave desert in California as smoothly as any aeroplane. Its fans argued that it would make launching scientific satellites and space stations much cheaper and easier now that a rocket did not have to be burnt up each time. Others pointed out that the costs of building space shuttle had been so great that it would be years before the USA got any money back on it.

Lift off: the space shuttle begins her maiden voyage.

Physicists find more pieces of the puzzle

EXCITING NEW DISCOVERIES were made in particle physics, the branch of science that tries to throw light on the origins and working of the universe by investigating the basic elements out of which all matter is made. During the year physicists in both India and the USA noted signs that protons could decay back into quarks. (Protons, along with electrons and neutrons are components of atoms and are themselves made up of even smaller particles called quarks.) If this could happen, then it might also be that quarks could then reconstitute themselves back into other kinds of basic matter like electrons and that all basic matter was interchangeable and had originated in the first place from a single source. If this was true, it would help to give scientists some idea of what happened to the universe in the first moment of its existence after the 'big bang', which, it was believed, lasted only the smallest fraction of a second.

High-speed train begins service in France

FRANCE'S NEW HIGH-SPEED TRAIN, the TGV, came into service on the Paris-to-Lyon route in September. Running on a specially-built straight track, it reached speeds of over 200 mph. The old journey time was cut in half to 2 hours 40 minutes. Britain, meanwhile, was experimenting with a type of train that tilted on corners so that it could run at high speeds on ordinary track. One of the new Advanced Passenger Trains – APTs – came into service on the London-to-Glasgow route in November but was withdrawn soon afterwards because of operating problems. Some experts doubted if the APT could ever really work.

New killer disease comes to light

DURING THE YEAR American doctors noticed that a serious lung infection – pneumocystis B – and a rare type of skin cancer had suddenly become far more common than usual among the gay populations of Los Angeles, San Francisco and New York. Normally these diseases struck only people whose immunity was low for some reason, such as people who had just had organ transplants. Why gay men should suddenly be affected no one knew.

Non-smokers at risk

A JAPANESE STUDY of lung-cancer victims, which was published in January, found that the wives of heavy smokers were twice as likely to die from the disease as the wives of non-smokers, even if they did not smoke themselves. Doctors called this 'passive smoking' and it gave an even stronger case to the anti-smoking lobby, which wanted to ban cigarettes from all public places.

1982

War in the

Argentinians invade the Falkland Islands

ON 2 APRIL ARGENTINIAN troops invaded the Falkland Islands and their Antarctic dependency of South Georgia. After three hours of fighting, the outnumbered garrison of British marines stationed there surrendered. Nearly 1800 people, mainly of British descent, lived on the small, windswept islands in the South Atlantic, which Argentina had long laid claim to.

Britain prepares to fight back

THE NEXT DAY – a Saturday – the House of Commons sat in emergency session and listened to Prime Minister Thatcher announce Britain's response. There was no question, she argued, of giving way to Argentina. A naval task force of 40 ships, carrying over 1000 crack troops, was already preparing to sail for the South Atlantic, over 8000 miles away. For once, most of the opposition agreed, although the government was strongly criticized for not having picked up the warning signs that Argentina was about to invade and thus being unprepared. The Foreign Secretary, Lord Carrington, resigned.

It is our duty to defend the right of the Falkland Islanders to stay British, if they wish to . . . Argentina has committed an act of naked aggression. If it is allowed to succeed, it will be a danger to people all over the world.
Denis Healey, Shadow Foreign Secretary, in the House of Commons, 3 April.

Britain receives widespread support

THE BULK OF WORLD OPINION lined up on the side of Britain. The United Nations Security Council met straight away in emergency session and rejected the Argentinian claim that all that had been done was to reclaim territory wrongly taken from her in the past. Britain's EEC partners announced an embargo on all trade with Argentina. The USA, which needed good relations with her South American neighbours, was more cautious. The Americans did, however, agree to allow Britain to use Ascension Island in the mid-Atlantic, about half-way between Britain and Argentina, as a refuelling post.

The Falkland Islands

As dawn breaks over the South Atlantic, Royal Marines line up for a weapons check aboard HMS Hermes, *the flagship of the British Task Force.*

Argentina rejoices

IN ARGENTINA there was widespread rejoicing at the recapture of what they called Las Malvinas. The divisions that had torn the country apart since the army took over in 1977 were forgotten.

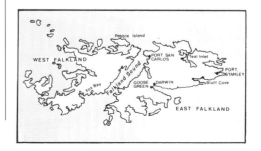

South Atlantic

Task force sails

IN THREE DAYS OF FRANTIC, round-the-clock activity, the force was assembled and sailed out of Portsmouth for the South Atlantic on 5 April, led by the aircraft carriers *Hermes* and *Invincible* and watched by thousands of cheering onlookers. The cruise liners, *Canberra* and *Queen Elizabeth II*, had been requisitioned as troop ships. General Galtieri, head of the military junta, swore that his troops would stay in Las Malvinas alive or dead. As the fleet sailed south, the likelihood that it would have to fight a real war, which no one had foreseen at the beginning of the year, became ever more likely.

Marines recapture South Georgia

BY 22 APRIL the task force was in the South Atlantic. A 200-mile exclusion zone was declared around the Falkland Islands. Any Argentinian ship within that zone would be subject to attack. Three days later a detachment of marines dropped by helicopter re-captured the island of South Georgia with few casualties. It was only a minor victory but was greeted in Britain with great excitement.

War at sea

ON 3 MAY British submarines sank the Argentinian cruiser *General Belgrano* with heavy loss of life among the sailors. The cruiser was 30 miles outside the exclusion zone at the time, but Britain claimed that she was heading towards the task force and that the sinking had been in 'self-defence'. Argentina retaliated the next day when HMS *Sheffield* was hit and sunk by a terrifying new missile: an Exocet, fired from an aeroplane flying too low to register on the ship's radar; 20 men died. The attack caused a wave of shock in Britain. Those who doubted whether the future of 1800 people on two bleak islands was worth losing real lives for now spoke out more boldly. At the same time some of the popular press began a campaign of hate against all Argentinians, which made many who supported the aims of the war feel ashamed.

We are at the very edge of a war whose end we cannot foresee. Nobody knows whether tactical nuclear weapons would be used and what the consequences might be . . . The gutter press have called us traitors, but I believe we represent the great majority of people who don't want to see any more killing.
Dame Judith Hart, at an anti-war rally at Hyde Park Corner, 9 May

Argentinians surrender

THE NEXT TARGET was the capital, Port Stanley. Progress was slow. On 8 June an attempt was made to shorten the cross-country trek by a behind-the-lines landing at Bluff Cove. Once again the landing craft were attacked by Argentinian jets before the men had time to disembark: 50 died and a further 55 were seriously wounded, many others suffered with horrific burns. Nonetheless, by the 13 June British troops had broken through to capture the three hill tops overlooking Port Stanley. The next day the Argentinians surrendered and it was all over. In Britain there was widespread rejoicing and not a little bragging. 'We had to do what we had to do', Mrs Thatcher told excited crowds outside 10 Downing Street that evening. 'Great Britain is great again.' Yet the war had cost nearly 1000 lives – 255 Britons and 652 Argentinians – and left others shattered.

Galtieri ousted

THREE DAYS AFTER the surrender, General Galtieri, who had been hailed as a hero only two months before, was ousted from power by fellow members of the military junta. The army stayed in control for the moment but whether it could live down the humiliation in the long run remained to be seen. The future of Argentina was now in the balance.

Troops land in the Falklands

ON 22 MAY British troops landed at San Carlos Bay in East Falkland and established a bridgehead there. They met no resistance on the ground but the landing was a close-run thing, for the landing ships were heavily attacked by Argentinian aircraft. Sixty men died.

The *Atlantic Conveyor* was hit by another Exocet. A week later the 2nd regiment of the Parachute Battalion met the first real opposition from enemy troops as they captured Goose Green and Port Darwin. They lost 17 men but took over 1400 prisoners.

World News

Gulf War hots up

THE GULF WAR was now in its third year. It hit the headlines once again in July when Iran launched a massive attack into Iraq, which threatened Baghdad itself. This was more than just revenge for the Iraqi invasion nearly two years before. Ayatollah Khomeini proclaimed it as the first stage in his *jihad* to spread the revolution throughout the Middle East. Among the prisoners taken by the Iraqis were boys as young as 12, who had been inspired to seek a martyr's death in war. Some of them even volunteered to walk through minefields before the attack to clear the way for regular soldiers. In the end, the attack petered out with heavy losses on both sides, but with Iran in such a fanatical mood no end to the war was in sight. It was estimated that the total number of deaths so far could be as many as 300,000.

Your Iranian brothers, in order to defend their country and push back the attacks on the enemies of Islam, have been forced to cross over into Iraq to save the oppressed Iraqi people. Rise up and install the Islamic government that you want.
From the broadcast by the Ayatollah Khomeini to the Iraqi people on the eve of the Iranian offensive, July 1982

Recession continues

THE RECESSION showed no sign of lifting and had now lasted longer than the one of the mid 1970s. The Third World debt burden reached crisis proportions, giving rise to talk about a collapse of the international financial system. Several Latin American countries, including Mexico, Argentina and Brazil, hovered on the brink of bankruptcy and had to be bailed out by the big banks.

The landscape of war: the destruction in both Iran and Iraq continued as no end to the Gulf War was in sight.

Walesa released

IN POLAND there was an uncomfortable stalemate. Martial law kept the country from total revolution but could not solve the nation's deeper problems. In October General Jaruzelski told an American magazine that he was on the horns of a dilemma. He could not rule without some co-operation from the restless people, yet failure to clamp down on any dissent would mean 'armed intervention by outsiders'. In November, though, he suddenly released Lech Walesa and other Solidarity leaders after nearly a year in detention. Whether this would help to solve Poland's deepening crisis remained to be seen.

US steps up aid to Central America

IN ACCORDANCE WITH its hardline stand against Communism, the Reagan administration had begun in 1981 to send military aid to right-wing groups in Latin America. Now this was stepped up dramatically to over $100 billion. Most of the aid went to the Contras in Nicaragua, who were fighting a guerilla war against the left-wing Sandanista government that had come to power in 1979, and to the anti-Communist government of El Salvador. This meddling in Central America worried many Americans. It seemed too much like the early stages of the entanglement in Vietnam and often involved backing governments that had as poor a human rights record as any Communist state. If the USA was in a fight to defend democracy, she had some strange allies.

'Falklands factor' boosts Tory popularity

BRITAIN'S ECONOMIC troubles continued throughout 1982, so too did fierce criticism of the government's handling of the crisis. At the beginning of the year Mrs Thatcher's future looked very doubtful. Her fortunes were transformed by the Falklands War, however, which converted her in many people's eyes into a heroine. Her iron determination to stick to a course of action once she had decided on it and her autocratic manner – characteristics that had made her unpopular with millions – suddenly seemed like assets. In a poll taken at the end of the year over half the country's voters now thought well of the government.

Israel invades Lebanon

SINCE THE MID 1970s the tiny country of Lebanon, home to a mixed population of Muslims and Christians plus thousands of Palestinian refugees, had been the cockpit for all the religious and political tensions of the Middle East. On 6 June tensions came to a head when Israel launched a fullscale invasion to clear out units of the Palestine Liberation Organization (PLO), which had been raiding northern Israel. After two months of street fighting, which reduced parts of Beirut to rubble and killed about 20,000 people, the PLO agreed to leave. No sooner had they gone than Christian militia units, who had worked with the Israelis, broke into the Sabra and Shatila refugee camps in West Beirut and massacred hundreds of civilians, many of them women and children. The Israelis denied complicity but few believed them.

Israel had gained what she came for but had lost many friends in the process. Even some Israelis now asked themselves whether their own survival justified some of the methods their government had been using. On 25 September 25,000 Israelis demonstrated in Tel Aviv against the massacres and demanded the resignation of Defence Minister, Ariel Sharon. In the autumn a multi-national force (MNF), including American marines, moved in to keep the peace in Beirut.

Trade Unions curbed

AN EMPLOYMENT BILL, aimed at curbing the power of the unions in Britain, was passed in October. It provided public funds for unions to finance secret ballots over wage disputes and outlawed closed shops and secondary picketing.

Russians bogged down in Afghanistan

AFTER THREE YEARS of fighting, the Soviet Union was no nearer clearing Afghanistan of the Mujaheddin, who used guerilla tactics and were supplied with arms by the USA.

They avoided taking on Soviet troops face to face but harassed and attacked in small groups, melting back again into the rugged countryside they knew so well. The main victims of the war were the ordinary people. Over two million of them – 12.5 per cent of the population – had fled across the border. No casualty figures for the Red Army were published.

Change of leadership in USSR

ON 10 NOVEMBER Leonid Brezhnev, Secretary of the Soviet Communist Party since 1964, died of a heart attack at the age of 75. During his 20 years at the top, the Soviet Union enjoyed stable government but the country underwent economic and political stagnation. Industry and agriculture were seriously underproductive, and queues and shortages became a part of daily life. All dissent was clamped down on.

Brezhnev's successor was Yuri Andropov, another elderly member of the Politburo.

Sport and the Arts

Hip hop makes it big

BLACK HIP HOP MUSIC became a real craze on both sides of the Atlantic. It was part of black street culture which also included breakdancing and graffiti from the slums of the Bronx in New York. Also known as 'rap', its distinctive feature was a hard, persistent background drum beat, while the words were spoken rather than sung, in rhythm with the beat, rather as a radio DJ might talk along with a record he was playing. The main theme of the lyrics was the moral and physical degradation suffered by blacks, especially young ones, in the inner city ghettoes. Sometimes the mood was despairing, as in Grandmaster Flash's *The Message*. Sometimes, as in Brother D's *How We Gonna Make a Black Nation Rise*, black people were told that they could, if they wanted to, break out of the ghetto mentality, with its culture of violence and drugs and build a new future for themselves.

You'll grow in the ghetto, you're second-rate
But your eye will sing a song of deep hate.
It's like a jungle out there.
Sometimes I wonder how I keep from goin' under.
The Message, Grandmaster Flash and the Furious Five

Italy springs a surprise

ITALY WERE SURPRISE WINNERS of the World Cup, played in Spain. In the first round they did not win any of their three matches and only scraped through to the next round on goal average. It was only in the final, where they beat West Germany 3-1, that they began to play well. England were knocked out in the quarter finals, as were Northern Ireland, who had surprised everyone by getting that far.

Video-game craze hits youth

THE CULT of the year was the video game, in which the player pitted his wits and quick reactions against a simulated situation on a screen. Over $5 billion and the equivalent in time of 75,000 years was spent playing machines in arcades in the USA alone. Many more games were played at home on computers that hooked up to the television set. Among the favourites were *Pac-man*, *Space Invaders* and *Defender*.

Mary Rose raised to the surface

THE MOST SPECTACULAR archaeological event in decades took place on 11 October, when the remains of a sixteenth-century warship *Mary Rose*, which had sunk in the Solent in 1545, was raised to the surface. This was the result of years of painstaking work by archaeologists and divers. It was planned to preserve the wreck and put her on public display in Portsmouth, along with hundreds of other relics found on her. These included weapons, drinking vessels and the bones of long-dead sailors.

Britain gets fourth TV channel

BRITAIN'S FOURTH TELEVISION CHANNEL went on the air on 2 November. One of its aims was to cater for minorities and broadcast the sort of programmes that other channels would not because they were not commercial enough. From the beginning Channel 4 had a rough time. It could not draw enough advertising revenue and its audiences were small. It was criticized in Parliament for putting on too many programmes geared to gays, Lesbians and feminists or that were too frank and free with their use of bad language. By the end of the year it seemed doubtful whether Channel 4 could survive in its present form.

Thompson sets new records

AT THE EUROPEAN ATHLETIC Championships held in Athens Daley Thompson set a new world record for the decathlon with 8744 points. He had now been unbeaten since 1978 and was the first man ever to hold the Olympic, European, Commonwealth and national titles and the world record all at the same time.

ET: *Steven Spielberg's creation of an extra-terrestrial charmed cinema audiences of all ages and pulled in record box office receipts.*

Science and Technology

Man receives artificial heart

IN DECEMBER an American dentist, Barney Clarke, whose own heart had failed, was wired up to the world's first artificial heart machine, invented by Dr William de Vries. This was a mechanical polyurethane and aluminium pump worked by electricity designed to do the work of a normal heart in pumping blood around the body. It meant that Mr Clark would have to be connected up to a power supply for the rest of his life – 'life tethered to a grocery cart', as he put it.

Lakes and forests in danger

A NEW DANGER to Earth's fragile environment came to public attention in 1982. This was the abnormally high levels of sulphuric and nitric acid to be found in rainfall in some areas. Acid rain, as it was called, polluted lakes and streams and sank into the soil, robbing it of nutrients. In the northern USA, Canada and Scandinavia, many lakes had already lost all their wildlife and forests were dying. Acid rain also ate away at stone and was damaging many of Europe's ancient monuments including St Paul's Cathedral and the Colosseum in Rome. The culprit, scientists concluded, was the fumes given off by power stations and smelting plants. Blown by the wind, acid rain was no respecter of international frontiers, and the worst affected countries were not always the worst offenders. The chances of anything being done quickly enough to stop further pollution seemed remote, for the greatest polluters, Britain and the USA, were reluctant to act.

The vicious circle of pollution.

Earth ringed by satellites

IN NOVEMBER the space shuttle launched its first satellites into orbit. There they joined the 1277 other operational ones that were already circling the earth – to say nothing of 1614 more that had long since fallen silent. The earth was now ringed with man-made objects, and although few people gave it much thought, much of daily life was unimaginable without the work they did. Satellites gave cheap and instantaneous communication around the world by telephone and television: without them the 1982 World Cup final could not have been watched by viewers in over 50 countries as it was being played. Satellites forecast the weather and gathered data about the state of the earth, even spotting deposits of minerals deep underground. More sinisterly, satellites were used to spy. It was rumoured that the USA's *Big Bird* could read the number plates on the Zil limousines used by high-ups in the Kremlin.

World given a grim warning

AN AMERICAN, Jonathan Schell, published a book called *The Fate of the Earth*, which shook the people who read it. In it he predicted that a nuclear war would spread a cloud over the planet causing a global 'nuclear winter' with months of sub-zero temperatures in the Northern hemisphere. When the cloud cleared, the damaged ozone layer would let in more ultra-violet rays than usual, causing cancers, blindness and genetic mutations. Civilization as we knew it would be dead. Those who had believed mankind could survive a nuclear war and rebuild were living in a fool's paradise.

If, in a nuclear holocaust, anyone hid himself deep enough under the earth and stayed there long enough to survive, he would emerge into a dying natural environment. . . There is no hole big enough to hide all of nature in.
From *The Fate of the Earth*, Jonathan Schell (Cape, 1982)

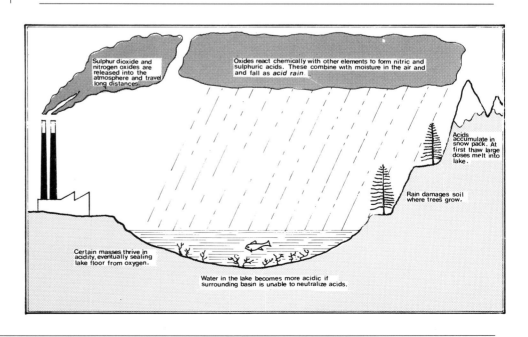

Sulphur dioxide and nitrogen oxides are released into the atmosphere and travel long distances.

Oxides react chemically with other elements to form nitric and sulphuric acids. These combine with moisture in the air and and fall as *acid rain*

Acids accumulate in snow pack. At first thaw large doses melt into lake.

Rain damages soil where trees grow.

Certain masses thrive in acidity, eventually sealing lake floor from oxygen.

Water in the lake becomes more acidic if surrounding basin is unable to neutralize acids.

Back to the

Cold War tensions rising

SINCE 1979 tensions between the two superpowers had risen so much that a nuclear war seemed more likely than it had at any time since 1962. Both sides blamed the other for breakdown.

Reagan condemns the Soviet Union as 'evil'

IN A HARD-HITTING SPEECH in Florida in March Reagan blamed the Soviet Union for the troubles of the modern world. This speech spread some alarm, for it seemed to signal that the USA no longer had any intention of even trying to rub along with the Russians and might even be thinking of an all-out crusade to crush Communism – a frighteningly dangerous prospect.

The Soviet Union is an evil empire . . . the focus of evil in the modern world . . . When evil is loose in the world, we are enjoined by scripture and the Lord Jesus to oppose it with all our might . . . let us not delude ourselves. The Soviet Union underlies all the unrest that is going on.
President Reagan in a speech made in Florida, 8 March

'Star Wars' takes world by surprise

SINCE THE MID 1970S TALKS had been going on in Geneva between the USA and USSR on reducing the arsenals of medium-range nuclear weapons they both kept in Europe. Little had been achieved, but the very fact that the talks took place at all gave hope to many. On 23 March, though, Reagan took his own country and the world by surprise when he announced on TV that scientists had thought up the ultimate weapon – the Strategic Defence Initiative or SDI, which the press nicknamed 'Star Wars'. This involved putting space stations into orbit designed to fire lasers capable of stopping enemy missiles before they even entered the earth's atmosphere. His critics claimed that this would only make nuclear war more likely.

The Soviet negotiators at Geneva refused to go on until Star Wars was abandoned. This Reagan would not do, and the Russians walked out on 23 November. For the first time in two decades there was no top-level contact between the superpowers.

The abrupt broadcasting of that unexamined project to the nation – and to the world – was, in my view, one of the most irresponsible acts by any head of state in modern times . . .
The Soviets would not sit idly by watching us build a shield behind which – as they saw it – we might safely launch a first strike . . . They would do what other nations have done when presented with a comparable threat – commit whatever resources were required to develop defensive weapons of their own . . . At the same time they would drastically increase the quality and quantity of their offensive weapons so that by the mass use of counter-measures, they would be able to overwhelm our defensive systems.
George Ball, *The War for Star Wars*, in *New York Review of Books*, 11 April. Ball had served four past presidents in foreign policy posts.

Arms race hots up

IN THE SAME MONTH, the first Cruise and Pershing 2 missiles moved into their bases in Europe. Both sides stepped up their military budgets for 1984, although they both already had the nuclear hardware to destroy the world many times over. American defence spending was now 50 per cent higher than it had been in 1979 and playing havoc with Reagan's promise to balance the federal budget. The Soviet budget was growing at between 4 and 8 per cent a year, faster than the overall economy. The cause of arms reduction, never very bright, now seemed to have no future at all.

Soviet Union shoots down civilian airliner

IN SEPTEMBER a Korean 747 airliner on route from New York to Seoul with 269 people on board strayed on to Soviet airspace and was shot down. Everyone in it died. The Russians refused to apologize, claiming that they had understandably mistaken it for an American spy plane. This action shocked American and world public opinion, but there were those who pointed out that it might be indicative of just how nervous of American

Cold War

Women peace protesters continue their protest even after Cruise missiles have been deployed at their Greenham base.

intentions the Russians had become. Whatever the truth, the thought of a jittery superpower was not very comforting.

Fear of nuclear holocaust grows

FEAR AMONG ORDINARY people that a nuclear war might actually happen one day was greater than at any time since the 1950s – made worse by a growing

suspicion that the aftermath of a nuclear holocaust might be even more horrific than most people believed. *The Fate of the Earth* came out in paperback, and in November 75 million Americans watched a TV drama, *The Day After*, about the horrendous consequences of a nuclear strike on a Kansas town. One of Reagan's undersecretaries caused a furore when he told a newspaper that the way to survive a nuclear attack was to hide in a hole, which made it look as if the government took the idea of a nuclear war far too lightly. A growing minority in Western Europe (less than a third of Britons, according to one survey), saw unilateral disarmament as the only answer. If the West took the intitiative and scrapped all her missiles, she would no longer be a target and might even persuade the Russians to do the same. The British Labour Party took this up in the 1983 election. Women from the peace camp of Greenham Common frequently broke into the military base to try and stop supplies entering. Although many were arrested and some imprisoned, the camp went on. On 22 October anti-nuclear rallies were held in many West European cities. Over 300,000 attended one in London and a million gathered in West German cities.

Dig a hole, cover it with a couple of doors, and then throw three feet of dirt on top. The dirt is really the thing that protects you. Everyone's going to make it if there are enough shovels to go around.
T. K. Jones, Reagan's Deputy Under-Secretary of Defence for Research and Engineering, in the Los Angeles *Times*, 29 March. Few people really accepted this official optimistic prognosis.

Price of oil plummets

THE PRICE OF CRUDE OIL fell sharply in 1983. After years of shortages, there was now a glut, and producers had to compete with each other for custom. OPEC, the Middle Eastern producers' cartel, which had once wielded more power than any national government, collapsed. For the industrialized economies of the West and their consumers, it was good news. Demand began to rise and unemployment dropped, especially in the USA. It was disastrous, however, for some oil producing countries like Mexico and Venezuala, who were already deeply in debt. It also led to a sharp drop in the value of sterling. In 1979 it had been worth $2-30, but it now dropped to $1-50 and was still falling at the end of the year.

Returning exile assassinated in broad daylight

IN THE PHILIPPINES, the government of Ferdinand Marcos, who had been in power since 1965, was becoming increasingly high-handed and corrupt. The USA, though, who had important air and naval bases on the island, backed him. The outside world took little notice of all this until August 1983, when Marcos' most outspoken opponent, Benigno Aquino, returned home from exile in spite of death threats against him. As soon as his plane touched down in Manila, he was taken off and shot in broad daylight in front of the press and TV cameras. Few people, at home or abroad, doubted that Marcos was behind it. Over 100,000 supporters turned out for Aquino's funeral, and the country erupted in riots and demonstrations.

Chaos in Lebanon

THE WAR IN THE LEBANON had left the country in chaos and at the mercy of factions, all armed to the teeth. The multi-national peace-keeping force found itself helpless. In the autumn lorries loaded with explosives were driven into the US marine barracks in Beirut and into an apartment block where French soldiers were sleeping. In total 297 foreign soldiers died. The culprits were probably members of Islamic Jihad, who believed that to die in a suicide attack was a martyr's death. Life for Westerners in Beirut became increasingly dangerous. A number of them disappeared during the year, presumably taken hostage.

Palestinian youths react to an Israeli army patrol helicopter as the hopes of peace in war-torn Lebanon evaporate.

Margaret Thatcher is welcomed by the troops on the Falklands. Her conduct of the war against Argentina greatly increased her popularity at home and helped the Tories to their second consecutive victory.

Military rule ends in Argentina

THE HUMILIATION of the Falklands defeat and economic crisis brought the Argentinian military junta down. In December Dr Raul Alfonsin became the country's first civilian President since 1976. He ordered an immediate investigation into all the human rights abuses rumoured to have taken place under the rule of the generals. Thousands of their opponents had disappeared without trace.

US Marines invade Grenada

THE USA CONTINUED to take a strong line against anything that smacked of Communism in Latin America and the Caribbean. In October marines were landed on the tiny island of Grenada to remove a left-wing government there that had seized power in a military coup. Most Americans approved, but many foreigners, including Mrs Thatcher, herself no friend of Communism, thought that the USA had acted too high-handedly.

Reagan did not get everything his own way, though, for Congress refused to grant all the funds he asked for to help the Contras in Nicaragua. Some Congressmen even argued that if the USA really wanted to prevent left-wing revolution in Latin America it might do better to tackle its root causes of poverty and oppression.

Mrs Thatcher triumphs again

BRITAIN'S ECONOMY was on the upturn too, although the recovery was unevenly spread. In the general election held in May, Mrs Thatcher's Tory government was swept back into office on a landslide. For Labour it was a disaster. They polled only 26 per cent of the vote, their lowest since 1935. Their stand on unilateral disarmament was one reason but more important may have been Britain's changing society. In the prosperous South whole new 'high-tech' industries like computers were opening up, and there was no such thing as a pure working class any more. In 1983, south of a line from the River Severn to the Wash, the Labour Party won only 29 seats, compared with 103 in 1966. In the autumn the Labour Party chose a new leader, Neil Kinnock. At 41 he was the youngest man ever to lead the Party.

Thatcher promises a Tory revolution

FLUSHED WITH HER VICTORY Mrs Thatcher promised the country a new revolution, which would sweep away much of what she called the 'Nanny state' and replace it with enterprise culture, where people would be encouraged to take risks, make money and take more responsibility for their own lives. Among the specific measures proposed were the privatization of nationalized industries including telecommunications, gas and airlines by selling shares in them to millions of ordinary people; the sale of council houses, so that everyone could one day become a home-owner; and more curbs on the trade unions. Nigel Lawson, an out-and-out monetarist, became Chancellor of the Exchequer.

Disappointment for SDP

THE SDP/LIBERAL ALLIANCE did not make the great electoral breakthrough it had hoped for, dashing hopes that the old two-party system might be on the way out.

After the election Roy Jenkins was replaced as leader of the SDP by David Owen, who had emerged during the campaign as the party's most forceful and convincing politician.

Breakfast-time TV comes to Britain

AMERICAN-STYLE breakfast-time TV went on the air in Britain for the first time. The BBC put on *Breakfast Time*, while ITV presented *Good Morning Britain*. Audience figures were low at first but were climbing by the end of the year. Channel 4 won much praise for its drama and current affairs programmes and began to pull in more viewers, although nowhere near as many as the other three stations.

British football accepts sponsorship

LIKE THE CINEMA, football in Britain suffered from falling attendances in the age of TV. Most clubs were struggling and many smaller ones were faced with bankruptcy. In other sports, like cricket or snooker, competitions sponsored by commercial firms were already commonplace. Now the Football League followed suit and signed its first-ever sponsorship deal. In return for money being pumped into the game, players would wear company logos on their shirts as a form of advertising. TV companies were given permission to screen a number of First Division and cup matches in full. After this, for the first time ever, at least one top match was played every Sunday. The League itself accepted £496,000 from the UK branch of a Japanese camera firm and renamed itself the Cannon League. Liverpool won their sixth league championship in nine years – a record. For the first time in six years, no British club won a European title.

Pop music lives up to its name

FOR THE FIRST TIME for a long while pop music was truly popular again, and stars like Boy George and Michael Jackson became household faces. Record sales soared. The main attraction was the catchiness of the songs and the colourful flamboyance of their style – recorded, of course, on video. Boy George, for instance, always wore female clothes and elaborate make-up. Many of the most popular groups, even in the USA, were British, like Culture Club, Wham and Duran Duran. But the biggest hit of the year was Michael Jackson's *Thriller* LP and video, which sold more copies than any other record ever. Established artists like The Rolling Stones, Paul Simon, Bob Dylan and David Bowie also did well.

Boy George, lead singer of Culture Club, whose long hair and make up symbolized the new flamboyance in pop music.

Top Sounds of 1983
Karma Chameleon – Culture Club
Thriller – Michael Jackson
Bad Boys – Wham
Let's Dance – David Bowie
Glory Days – Bruce Springsteen
Synchronicity album – Police

Sportswear in fashion

THE BIG FASHION HIT of the year, which looked like being around for a long time, was the two-piece jogging suit, which up to now had been worn mainly for running. Suddenly they could be found in all sorts of materials from practical towelling to silk and could be worn for almost anything from just lounging around to going to parties.

British cinema in decline

BRITISH CINEMA AUDIENCES dropped to 60 million, 26 per cent down on the year before. This drop had been going on since the arrival of television but was now being speeded up by the popularity of VCRs. Few households had owned one in 1980 but now over 30 per cent did. Video rental shops were becoming a common sight in every town. Popular movies like *ET* and *The Return of the Jedi* were available on video almost as soon as they were released, although this was illegal. This was not just a revolution in the way people organized their leisure but also a threat to the whole film-making industry. Without a steady income from cinema audiences, it would be difficult to raise the money to make new films. In spite of this, a British film *Gandhi*, directed by Richard Attenborough, won a record eight Oscars in this year's Academy Awards.

Recording breakthrough

THE FIRST DIGITAL RECORDS and players, invented in Japan, went on sale in the USA. Known as compact discs, they worked by translating sound into numbers, which were stored in pits embedded on the disc. When they were played, a laser beam read the numbers and translated them back into sound. Their makers claimed that they could not be scratched or damaged and nor would they ever wear out. The sound was better, too, as there was no distortion. Compact discs were much more expensive, though, than ordinary records.

Scientists warn of greenhouse effect

REPORTS BY THE National Association of Sciences in the USA voiced a fear that so much carbon dioxide was now being given off by burning fossil fuels like coal and oil and cutting down trees that it could not all escape from the earth's atmosphere. As the gas built up, it acted as a suntrap, letting the sun's heat in but not allowing it out again, like glass in a greenhouse. As a result the temperature of the earth was rising. The end result would be the melting of the polar ice cap and catastrophic climatic changes, including the flooding of coastal plains and drought in inland areas. Whole nations like Bangladesh might disappear.

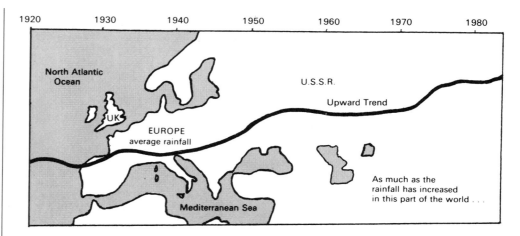

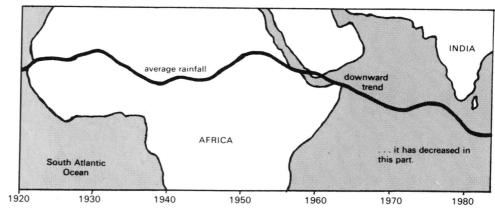

The mirror image: as average rainfall in Europe has risen, the average in Africa has dropped, with catastrophic effects.

AIDS spreading

THE MYSTERY DISEASE that was attacking America's gay population continued to spread. There were now 60 new cases diagnosed every month in the USA, and cases started cropping up in European cities as well. It now had a name – acquired immune deficiency syndrome or AIDS – but there was still no clear idea what caused it.

World's climate disturbed

SOME EXPERTS BELIEVED that 1983 gave the world a foretaste of what was to come. Over 40 countries were seriously affected by drought or floods. African states like Ethiopia and the Sudan were struck by famine. Thousands were killed in floods in Bolivia, Ecuador and Peru, while in Australia a prolonged drought caused devastating bush fires. Hiccups in the earth's climate were nothing new – they had been recorded throughout history. The trouble now was that no one knew how much was natural and how much was man-made.

Man with artificial heart dies

BARNEY CLARKE died in March after 112 days tethered to his artificial heart. The machinery itself had functioned well but Clarke's own body had gradually broken down under the strain. Much of the time he had been comatose and died in the end of kidney failure. The general opinion was that medical technology was not up to replacing human tissue with a machine – not yet anyway – and that the experiment should not be tried again.

A surge of pride and patriotism

THE EVENTS of the 1970s – from Vietnam to Watergate, from the Iranian hostage crisis to the recession – had dented Americans' confidence in themselves and their future. The nation that in 1960 had thrilled to President Kennedy's call to go out and bring prosperity and justice to the rest of the world felt humiliated and demoralized. Since the early 1980s, though, this had began to change, and by 1984 it was obvious to all – at home and abroad – that a new mood of pride and patriotism was sweeping the nation. One look at the number of US flags flying outside ordinary homes was proof of that.

I haven't found anyone who doesn't feel good about being an American right now.
From interviews in *Time*, 24 September

US economy booming

ONE REASON for the optimism was the booming economy. In the first half of the year output rose by an astounding 8 per cent. Unemployment dropped too. Over the last two years six million new jobs had been created. With inflation still low, real living standards were rising fast, reviving the old American Dream that anyone who worked hard could build a good life for themselves and their families. The dollar, in trouble in 1979, was now the world's strongest currency. Not everyone did well out of the boom, though. The poor – about one-fifth of the population – gained nothing from tax cuts and the strong dollar and were hard hit by cuts in federal spending. An epidemic of cocaine addiction was sweeping through the inner cities, giving rise to a new crime wave and blighting thousands of lives. Pockets of unemployment remained in the old smokestack industry areas. And, with defence expenditure at a record high, the budget deficit was still growing. For 1984 it was projected to be over $400 million.

Reagan symbolizes the new mood

SYMBOL OF THE NEW America was President Ronald Reagan himself. His critics accused him of seeing the world in black and white, which might plunge Americans and everyone else into a fatal conflict with the USSR. At home he ignored the problems of the poor, the blacks and the inner cities, just as he ignored the budget deficit. To most Americans, though, none of this mattered. Under Reagan's presidency life had got better, and the USA had stood up for herself once again on the world stage. The old-fashioned values he spoke of and symbolized, like patriotism and religious faith, were what they wanted to believe about themselves.

There is renewed energy and optimism throughout the land. America's back – standing tall, looking to the 80s with courage, confidence and hope . . . America's new strength, confidence and purpose are carrying hope and opportunity far from our shores. A world economic recovery is underway. It began here.
Reagan's *State of the Union* message, delivered to Congress, 25 January

Victory: Reagan, with his wife, Nancy, beside him, thanks his loyal supporters after his second successful presidential election campaign.

rides high

Glittering spectacle at Los Angeles

THE 1984 OLYMPIC GAMES were held in Los Angeles, with 140 nations taking part. They were boycotted by the USSR and Eastern Europe, however, in retaliation for the American boycott of the 1980 Moscow Olympics. For the first time, the staging was left to private contractors, and everything went perfectly, from the relay that carried the torch across the continent to the spectacular, Hollywood-style closing ceremony.

In the absence of competition from the Russians and East Germans, American athletes dominated events, winning 83 gold medals. These results were greeted with an outburst of national pride and patriotism.

Not everyone, though, liked what they saw at Los Angeles. The games, which made a huge profit for their organizers, were often too commercial – even to the extent of selling the right to carry the Olympic torch along a section of its route. Others felt that the spirit of the games, which were supposed to symbolize international co-operation, had been soiled by too much crude patriotism. ABC TV, for example, which paid $225 million for the television rights, concentrated far too much on the achievements of American athletes and ignored almost everyone else.

The Los Angeles Olympics, the first to be run as a private, profit-making enterprise, exuded all the glamour and panache of a Hollywood movie.

Born in the USA

THE BIG HIT-RECORD of the year was *Born in the USA* by the rock-singer Bruce Springsteen, which the Reagan administration adopted as a sort of theme tune. In fact, it was obvious that no one involved had bothered to listen to the words properly. Far from being a celebration of the American way of life, the song was a lament for the hardships and disillusion suffered by a working-class Vietnam veteran from one of the old smokestack regions. None of this, though, dented the record's popularity as a symbol of the New America.

Born down in a dead man's town
The first kick I took was when I hit the ground
You end up like a dog that's been beat too much
Till you spend half your life just covering up.

Born in the USA
I was born in the USA
Opening lines of *Born in the USA* by Bruce Springsteen

Reagan wins landslide election victory

REAGAN STOOD for re-election in November. His opponent, Walter Mondale, broke new ground by choosing a woman – Geraldine Ferraro – as his running mate. Mondale put forward the case of the one-fifth of Americans who had not done well out of the Reagan boom and hinted that taxes might have to be raised to help the poor. Few Americans wanted to hear this, and Reagan swept home with a huge majority, winning 49 out of the 50 states. One new feature of the campaign was the emergence of the first serious black candidate, the Revd. Jesse Jackson. Although Jackson did not win the Democratic nomination, he persuaded more blacks to turn out to vote than ever before. Many hoped this would persuade both parties to take the needs of black people more seriously in the future.

World News

Mrs Gandhi shot

ON 31 OCTOBER Mrs Gandhi, the Prime Minister of India, was shot dead by two Sikh members of her bodyguard in the gardens of her house in Delhi. This was in revenge for events on 5-6 June, when the army stormed the Golden Temple at Amritsar, holiest of Sikh shrines, which was being used by Sikh militants (who wanted independence for their state of Punjab) as a store-house for weapons. An estimated 712 Sikhs died and the shrine was damaged.

Mrs Gandhi was succeeded by her son Rajiv. In the wave of anti-Sikh riots that broke out afterwards, over 1000 people died, most of them innocent Sikh families who were attacked and murdered in their homes.

Britain and China agree over Hong Kong's future

BRITAIN'S COLONY of Hong Kong was a tiny island of capitalism just off the coast of China, where life was very different to that on the Communist mainland. Its inhabitants were worried about what would happen when the British lease expired in 1997 and the Chinese took over. Talks had been going on between China and Britain since 1982, and in September agreement was reached. Although sovereignty would pass to China on schedule in 1997, Hong Kong would retain a large degree of self-government and would keep her own way of life for at least the next 50 years. This was probably the best deal Hong Kong could hope for, but nevertheless it left many people rather nervous. Who knew who would be in power in Beijing over the next half century and whether they could be relied on to keep their word?

Another Soviet leader dies

SOVIET LEADER ANDROPOV died on 13 February after only 15 months in office. For the last six of them he had been so ill that he had not been seen in public. His successor was another old and sick man, Konstantin Chernenko, aged 72. There was little chance that he, any more than Andropov, would have the time or energy to deal with the USSR's pressing domestic and foreign problems, including the war in Afghanistan, now in its fifth year and with no end in sight.

Reagan and Congress clash over Nicaragua

IN APRIL IT CAME TO LIGHT that President Reagan, frustrated by Congress's refusal to give whole-hearted backing to his support for the Nicaraguan Contras, had allowed the CIA to send secret aid. The year before they had even mined some of Nicaragua's harbours to prevent Soviet aid reaching the Sandanistas. Congress was livid at this flouting of its authority. Even right-wing Republicans like Barry Goldwater, who were as staunchly anti-Communist as the President, thought this was going too far and might put the USA on the road to another Vietnam. Congress consequently cut off all aid to the Contras.

Famine hits Ethiopia again

FOR TWO YEARS the rains had failed in sub-Saharan Africa, causing famine to spread in a wide swathe from Mali in the west to Mozambique in the east. Worst hit was Ethiopia. Over 100,000 had already died, and millions more were crowded into refugee camps, where food and medicine were scarce and epidemics spread. Millions faced almost certain death. In October a BBC TV film of the refugee camp at Korem was screened. Its impact was so harrowing that aid began flooding in from the West. By the end of the year, though, little had reached the stricken areas.

IRA bomb wrecks Tory conference hotel

AT 3 A.M. on the morning of 12 October a bomb went off in a bedroom of the Grand Hotel in Brighton, where the Prime Minister and most of the Cabinet were staying during their party conference. The explosion wrecked five floors, including Mrs Thatcher's suite, although she escaped unhurt. Five people died and others were seriously injured, including Industry Minister Norman Tebbit and his wife. Responsibility was claimed by the IRA.

Gulf War spreads

THE IRANIANS began mining the waters of the Gulf and the narrow Straits of Hormuz in order to stop Western tankers carrying oil out of the Gulf States, who backed Iraq. Ships of the US Navy were sent to guard American tankers. The chances that this local war would spread into an international conflict were growing.

Long pit strike begins

IN BRITAIN a miners' strike began on 10 March and was still going on at the end of the year. Although the immediate issue at stake was the Coal Board's plan to close 20 pits, underlying this was the bitterness that working-class communities felt towards a government that seemed intent on writing off Britain's old heavy industries and condemning whole regions to decay.

The strike soon erupted into bitterness and violence between miners who went on strike and those who did not. Teams of flying pickets were sent from militant areas to picket the working mines. Violent clashes with the police followed. At Orgreave coking plant a pitched battle took place in May, in which 41 policemen and 28 miners were injured.

By the end of the year there was deadlock. In spite of the hardship they were suffering, most miners remained solidly behind the strike. Yet the strike had not brought the country to its knees, as the National Union of Miners (NUM) leader, Arthur Scargill, had promised it would do. The miners received little help from the other big unions: the railway workers went on carrying coal and the steelworkers continued making steel.

Britain's new class war

This is the strike to end all strikes. If we win, we have won for all the working class. If they beat us, the working class loses its life-style.
Miner's wife from Barnsley, Yorks, quoted in *Time*, 24 December

You will be able to look back in the knowledge that you can say with pride to your sons and daughters, 'I took part in the greatest struggle in trade union history'. If you hold out now, you will not always be poor.
Arthur Scargill, to Yorkshire miners, 19 December

Two years ago we fought the enemy without; but the enemy within we are facing now is just as dangerous. We must not back down.
Mrs Thatcher to Tory Party back-benchers, 17 October

The miners united: this scene of miners marching confidently belies the bitter divisions within the industry that the strike caused.

Pop stars sing for Ethiopia

THE MOST MEMORABLE MUSICAL happening of 1984 was Band Aid, the get-together in December of Britain's top rock stars to help the starving in Ethiopia. Among those taking part were Sting, Phil Collins, Simon le Bon (of Duran Duran), Boy George and George Michael (of Wham). Organized by former Boomtown Rats lead singer, Bob Geldof and Midge Ure, ex-lead singer of Ultravox, they produced a single called *Do They Know It's Christmas?*, which shot straight to the top of the charts. All the proceeds went to famine relief.

Frankie causes shock waves

THE SURPRISE HIT GROUP of the year was Frankie Goes to Hollywood. Their first record, *Relax*, a celebration of gay sex, had been banned by the BBC at the end of 1983. It shot to Number 1! Their next record, *Two Tribes*, was accompanied by a video showing Reagan and Chernenko punching and gouging each other. It finished with the world exploding. Frankie were billed as the first genuine protest group since the punks. Tee-shirts with *Frankie Say* slogans became fashionable. There were suspicions, though, that the group were really only the product of a clever manager, Paul Morley, who had seen a gap in the pop market and groomed them to fill it. Whether they would last only time would tell. Some of the big groups of 1983 like Culture Club and Wham faded in 1984 but Michael Jackson's *Thriller* went on selling. By the end of the year it had sold over 45 million copies worldwide.

FRANKIE SAY RELAX

FRANKIE SAY ARM THE UNEMPLOYED

Two slogans from the Frankie tee-shirts

A new word comes into the language

A NEW WORD came into the English language: 'Yuppie'. Originating in the USA, it was used to describe the young whizz-kids who were doing well out of the enterprise culture. It stood for 'young, upwardly-mobile professional'. Certain expensive consumer goods such as Porsche and BMW cars, designer clothes like Calvin Klein, Filofaxes and car telephones became status symbols of Yuppie culture.

The South-African-turned-British runner Zola Budd, running characteristically barefoot.

New programmes on British TV
The Jewel in the Crown, Granada's 13-part adaptation of Paul Scott's work *The Raj Quartet*
Threads, a drama about a nuclear attack on Britain
Spitting Image, a political satire with puppets
Strangers and Brothers, an adaptation of C. P. Snow's novels

Cable TV comes to Britain

THE FIRST CABLE TV channels opened in Britain and France. They were run by independent companies, and anyone who had a cable run to their house could pay to receive whichever channels they liked. The old monopoly of the BBC and ITV over what appeared on the screen had ended. Fans of cable TV claimed that it would increase freedom of choice for the viewer. Others thought it would lower the quality of British TV. Ironically, this year the output on BBC and ITV was of an unusually high quality, and British programmes won a number of awards at international festivals.

Zola Budd affair causes outrage

ZOLA BUDD was a 17-year-old South African girl who in January broke the world 5000 m record. As a South African, though, she could not run in international competitions. In April the *Daily Mail* brought her to Britain and rushed through her citizenship, so that she could run for Britain in the Los Angeles Olympics that summer. Many people thought this whole episode was immoral. When she did run in the Olympic 3000 m that summer, it ended in disaster when she accidentally tripped up American Mary Decker.

Record on ice

THE MOST NOTEWORTHY event of the 1984 Olympics for Britain took place not in Los Angeles but at the Winter Olympics in Sarajevo. With a stunning dance routine to the music of Ravel's *Bolero*, British skaters, Jayne Torvill and Christopher Dean, won a score of all 6s, which no one had ever done before.

Daily life being changed by the microchip

SINCE THE MICROCHIP revolution began in the 1970s, the technology had developed so rapidly and the costs come down so fast that the chip and the machines that ran by it had become part of daily life – almost before people realized it. VCRs, personal stereos, digital watches, automatic cash dispensers, calculators large and small – the list was endless. Many people now owned their own personal computer or word processor. Scientists foretold the day when many of the dangerous or repetitive jobs in heavy industry would be done by microprocessors that would overcome human handicaps. Work was going on, for instance, on a telephone for the deaf that would print out whatever the voice at the other end was saying.

If the automobile industry had improved its technique at the same rate computer science has, it would now be turning out Rolls Royces that cost no more than $70 a piece.
The pace of development is roughly akin to going from the Wright brothers' first aeroplane to the space shuttle in a decade.
From *Time* magazine, 3 January

Baby given baboon's heart

ONE OF THE MOST extraordinary transplant stories happened in California in October. A 15-day-old baby was given a baboon's heart in a five-hour operation to replace a defective heart. This was the first time that a baboon's heart had been used in this way. The operation raised important ethical questions about organ transplanting. A hospital spokesman said that 'she will live a long life with this heart'. He was wrong. The baby died 21 days later and the experiment was not repeated.

Communications revolution set to begin

ONE APPLICATION of the new technology took off in 1984, when British Telecom began replacing its electronic telephone cables (which had not changed much since the telephone was invented at the end of the last century) with optic fibres. These were hair-thin glass fibres that carried signals coded as a pulse of light. A single fibre could carry many conversations faster and more accurately than the old system. On 31 December the world's first cellular radio network – Vodafone – opened in London. This was a network of short-range radio transmitters and receivers that connected mobile telephones to national and international lines. The transmitters automatically selected the right frequency for each call and routed them through the nearest receiver, changing it as the caller moved. The age of cordless and car telephones had arrived.

AIDS virus discovered

SCIENTISTS IN FRANCE and the USA identified a virus – known as HTLV or LAV – as the cause of AIDS. It could be spread through sexual intercourse with an infected person, contaminated blood or dirty needles, but not through everyday contact. It would no longer do just to write it off as the 'gay plague'. Everyone was vulnerable. More and more cases were turning up among heterosexuals, drug-users and haemophiliacs, who had been given transfusions of infected blood. Babies with AIDS were being born to mothers who had the disease.

Thousands die in poison gas leak

THE DARKER SIDE of modern technology was seen at Bhopal in India in December, when an American-owned chemical plant leaked methyl isocynate, a highly toxic gas, into the air. At least 2000 people died and a further 200,000 were affected. Some were blinded, others had damaged kidneys or lungs. No one knew if any of them would ever recover.

As the Indian government declared Bhopal a disaster area, it was revealed that similar leaks, though on a much smaller scale, had occurred at the factory on four previous occasions.

Pregnant women warned off VDUs

PREGNANT WOMEN were warned not to work on Visual Display Units (VDUs) following the publication of surveys commissioned by the Civil Service Trade Unions over an eight-year period up to 1982. The surveys, carried out by the Civil Service Medical Advisory Service, showed that the level of radiation transmitted from the screens was unexpectedly high, and that there was therefore an increased chance of miscarriage for women who spent a sizable proportion of their day in front of the screens. Many other experts were sceptical of the evidence, however, and pointed out that there was a similar level of radiation emitted from televisions.

1985 World Swept by

Acts of terrorism rarely out of the headlines

SINCE THE EARLY 1970s stories of hijacking, hostage-taking and bombing had rarely been out of the news headlines. While most people condemned those responsible for such acts as nothing but murderers, the terrorists themselves argued that it was often the only way they could bring their case to world attention. 1985 was a particularly bad year for terrorism and gave rise to some disturbing new developments, including a number of outrages around the world that seemed to have no purpose other than mindless revenge against racial or religious opponents. At the forefront was a new wave of Islamic hatred and vengeance against Westerners, especially Americans.

A masked hijacker emerges from the TWA jet.

More bombings and kidnappings in Lebanon

THE MNF HAD WITHDRAWN from the Lebanon in 1984, and in the spring the Israelis went too, although they kept a security zone along the southern frontier and from time to time bombed villages suspected of harbouring Palestinian terrorists. The battle between the factions went on. Over 2000 were killed in fighting between Amal and Hezbollah in Tripoli in September. Westerners continued to be targets, although often it was far from clear exactly what the purpose of attacks on them were – other than a spirit of revenge against the West for all that had happened in the past. Six more American citizens, plus four British and French went missing in Beirut. One, William Buckley, was killed. In October four officials from the Soviet embassy, which had previously been immune from attack, were kidnapped. One was killed before the other three were released.

We declare that in revenge for the blood of our martyrs, we announce the execution of William Buckley after he has been tried and found guilty of involvement in American crimes around this world.
Statement by Islamic Jihad, 4 October

Britons freed from Libya

AT THE BEGINNING OF FEBRUARY Terry Waite, the special representative of the Archbishop of Canterbury, travelled to Libya to plead for the release of four Britons who had been held hostage there for nine months – victims of Gadaffi's campaign of hate against the West. His mission succeeded, and the captives were released on the 6th. Rumour had it that Gadaffi, a devout Muslim who was contemptuous of the materialistic values of the West, was impressed by the depth of Waite's own Christian faith. The 6 ft 7 in bearded Waite, who had been unknown to the general public only a few weeks before, was on his way to becoming one of the heroes of the year.

Wave of Terrorism

TWA Jet Hijacked

IN JUNE A TWA PLANE flying from Athens to Rome was hijacked by members of the Islamic Jihad, who demanded in exchange for the hostages the release of 700 of their comrades held by Israel. One American passenger – a young sailor – was killed straight away. Most of the hostages were released soon after, but the 39 Americans on board were still held. President Reagan, who had once sneered at Carter's inability to free the Teheran embassy hostages, ruled out an armed rescue attempt as too dangerous. For two tense weeks the unfortunate passengers were shuttled backwards and forwards between Beirut and Algeria as frantic negotiations went on behind the scenes. On 30 June the hostages were finally set free, and Israel quietly released the prisoners the next day. For Reagan, who had found himself as helpless as Carter had once been, it was a great humiliation. He vowed it would not happen again.

We and our similarly threatened friends must see what actions, military or otherwise, can be taken to end this increasingly violent, indiscriminate but purposeful threat to humanity . . . we will not rest until justice has been done. Terrorists be on notice. We will fight back against you in Lebanon and elsewhere.
Ronald Reagan in a TV broadcast to the American people, 1 July

Hundreds die as Air India plane blows up

TO SOME EXTENT PASSIONS died down in India. The new Prime Minister, Rajiv Gandhi, drew up a compromise granting a limited degree of autonomy to the Sikh community and promising to repair the damaged temple. This was accepted by most moderate Sikhs. Then in June an Air India Boeing 747 en route from Toronto to London crashed into the sea off the coast of Ireland. All 325 on board were killed. The disaster happened so suddenly – the plane simply disappeared from the radar without warning – that the only possible cause could have been a bomb, although no one ever proved it beyond doubt. The culprits were suspected to be Sikh extremists marking their protest against what they saw as a sellout by their leaders in India.

The now-familiar figure of Terry Waite, accompanied by his protectors, on his peace mission to Libya.

The USA strikes back

IN OCTOBER MEMBERS OF THE PLO hijacked a cruise liner, the *Achille Lauro*, in the Mediterranean, with 454 passengers on board. If 50 Palestinians held in Israeli jails were not released, they threatened to blow up the ship and everyone in it. One passenger, an elderly Jewish American, Leon Klinghoffer, who was confined to a wheelchair, was shot and his body thrown overboard. When the hijackers finally surrendered to the Egyptians on the promise of a safe conduct to friendly Tunisia, the USA took action. The plane flying the Palestinians to safety was intercepted by American jet fighters and forced to land in Sicily. Attempts by US troops to seize the terrorists and take them back to the USA for trial were then thwarted by the Italians, who insisted on their own right to arrest them. A few days later the terrorist leader, Mohammed Abbas, was allowed quietly to escape.

15 die in airport attacks

ON 27 DECEMBER PLO terrorists attacked the El Al ticket desks at Rome and Vienna airports, killing 15 people – and injuring many more. In a shoot-out with airport security staff that followed four terrorists were killed and the rest wounded. The survivors claimed that the attacks had been in revenge for a recent Israeli attack on a Palestinian camp, but the official PLO under Yasser Arafat denied having anything to do with it.

Gorbachev becomes new Soviet leader

CHERNENKO DIED IN MARCH. His successor was Mikhail Gorbachev, at 54 the youngest Soviet leader since the Second World War. His style of leadership was quite different from anything seen in Russia for many years. He frequently left his car to walk about the streets among ordinary people and listened as much as he talked. In one of his first major speeches, he sharply criticized the stagnation of the Brezhnev era.

Within months many of the old generation of Party officials had been swept away to make places for younger men.

Gorbachev and Reagan meet at Geneva

The modern world has become too fragile for wars and a policy of force . . . it is no longer possible to win an arms race, or a nuclear war for that matter.
Mr Gorbachev to Party workers in Moscow, 23 September

From the beginning, Gorbachev talked of his dream of a world without nuclear weapons. Reagan took up the challenge. In November the two men met at Geneva, where they had more than five hours of discussions on their own, with only interpreters present. No agreements were signed, and the gulf between them remained wide. None-theless, they liked and respected each other. 'The chemistry worked', Reagan told reporters afterwards. They agreed that talks on reducing nuclear arms should begin right away and that they would speak to each other's people directly on TV on New Year's Day 1986. The 'spirit of Geneva' – as the press called it – was quite a turnaround after the tensions of the past few years. Gorbachev himself had become something of a media star in the West.

The Secretary of the Soviet Communist Party, Mikhail Gorbachev, heralded a new style of Soviet leadership.

South Africa explodes

CHRONIC UNREST among South Africa's black population flared up into widespread violence especially against black officials like policemen and mayors, who were seen as collaborators. One horrific new weapon was the 'necklace', a tyre filled with petrol that was put round the neck of the victim and set alight. Most of the violence was spontaneous – the result of years of pent-up frustrations – but there was also a marked increase in planned guerilla attacks like car bombings. For the first time the privileged white population was put in danger. On 23 December a bomb planted in a shopping centre in Natal killed five.

In July the government declared a state of emergency, accompanied by wholesale arrests of anyone suspected of being involved in violence. The media were accused of fanning the unrest up and forbidden to show or publish any pictures of disturbances. To many people, including some whites, it was fast becoming clear that repression alone would not work. Calm would never come to South Africa until the unjust system of apartheid was swept away. President Botha hinted that his TV speech, scheduled for 15 August, would announce widespread reforms. It did not. Even moderate black leaders like Archbishop Desmond Tutu began to talk about the need to use violence. South Africa seemed to be on the verge of armed revolution.

Deaths (Sept – Dec 1985)	965	
Worst month – Aug 1985	163 died	
Buildings destroyed		
through arson	920	schools
	33	churches
	17	clinics
	639	shops
	2528	houses
	5054	buses
	5338	cars
Total cost of damage	**R 100 million**	

Times figures on South Africa, published 20 December 1985

Britain 1985 – a divided society?

WHILE THE ECONOMY as a whole continued to recover, unemployment remained above the three-million mark all year, condemning whole urban areas in the North and London to poverty and decay. It seemed to many as if Britain was indeed a deeply-divided nation, with a growing gulf between the lifestyles and living standards of the prosperous South and the impoverished North, between those with work and those without, many of whom were young or black. In October serious rioting broke out once again in Liverpool and London. The main targets were the police, and most of the rioters were young. On the Broadwater Farm estate in Tottenham a policeman was beaten to death by an angry crowd. How much this had to do with years of deprivation and rising unemployment, especially among black teenagers, no one knew.

Blacks continue to protest in Soweto against the injustice of the Apartheid regime despite the state of emergency.

Marcos under pressure

THE UNPOPULARITY of President Marcos continued to mount. He and his wife, Imelda, were accused of stashing huge sums of money away abroad for their own use – $650 million, according to one American newspaper. The campaign against him was led by Mrs Corazon Aquino, widow of the man murdered in 1983, who had never taken part in politics before.

Miners' strike ends

AFTER THE NEW YEAR the miners' strike in Britain began to crack. On 5 March, only a few days short of a year after it was started, it was called off. Although the miners were proud of the heroic stand they had taken to save their jobs and communities, nothing could hide the fact that they had been beaten in the end. The Coal Board's programme of pit closures went ahead as planned, with the loss of 30,000 jobs. After this it was doubtful if any other trade union would dare take on the redoubtable Mrs Thatcher and her government. The once-powerful British unions had been cowed.

New attempt to bring peace to Ulster

ON 15 NOVEMBER Britain and the Irish Republic signed the Anglo-Irish agreement, which it was hoped would help to end a decade and a half of violence and bloodshed in Northern Ireland. Its main feature was to make it easier for Britain to extradite wanted IRA men who had slipped over the border into the Republic and have them sent back to the North for trial. For the time being, though, the spasmodic violence that had troubled the province since 1969 went on.

Sport and the Arts

41 die as English football fans go on the rampage

THE HOOLIGANISM of some English football fans abroad, which had made them loathed and feared throughout Europe, came to a tragic climax before the European Cup Final between Liverpool and Juventus at the Heysel Stadium in Brussels on 29 May. The trouble flared up when Liverpool supporters, some armed with metal or concrete posts they had torn up, charged towards a group of Italian fans. The fence separating them collapsed,

Scenes of anguish after the collapse of a wall at Heysel stadium.

and in the fighting that followed 41 people were trampled or crushed to death and hundreds were injured. Video film of the riot left no doubt that English fans were to blame. Four days later UEFA put an indefinite ban on English clubs playing in Europe.

Heysal was not the only tragedy for English football in a year when events off the field overshadowed those on it. On 11 May a fire in the stand at the Bradford City ground killed 55.

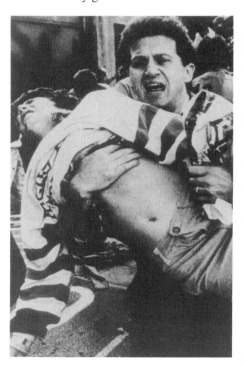

17-year-old wins Wimbledon

THE SURPRISE WINNER of the men's singles at Wimbledon was 17-year-old unseeded Boris Becker of West Germany who beat John McEnroe in the final. Tennis now had a new idol. In the women's game Martina Navratilova went on winning, beating Chris Evert Lloyd to win the singles at Wimbledon for the fourth year running.

Records tumble

PERHAPS THE MOST REMARKABLE sporting event of the year took place in middle-distance running. In five breathtaking weeks in the summer Steve Cram of Britain and Said Aouita of Morocco broke the world 1500 m record four times between them. On one day in Nice in July they both broke it in the same race. By the end, the record stood at 3 minutes 26.46 seconds held by Aouita. Aouita and Cram had now replaced Coe and Ovett as the world's top middle-distance runners.

Baseball record broken

ON 11 SEPTEMBER Pete Rose of the Cincinnati Reds broke Ty Cobb's record, which had stood since 1928, for the greatest number of hits in major league baseball.

Rock Stars go into Politics

AFTER THE EXAMPLE of Band Aid, the idealism that had often been a feature of rock music was revived. In July two international 16-hour pop festivals called Live Aid, again organized by Bob Geldof, were held in Wembley Stadium, London, and JFK Stadium, Philadelphia. They were broadcast live to 1.5 billion people around the world and raised £40 million for famine relief in Africa. Among the performers, who played for free, were Queen, Dire Straits, David Bowie, Madonna and Mick Jagger. In Britain Billy Bragg organized Red Wedge, to persuade young people to vote Labour at the next election. Robert Wyatt and Jerry Dammers of The Specials took up the anti-apartheid cause and co-operated with students from Namibia to make a single *Wind of Change*. The proceeds went to SWAPO.

Frankie Goes to Hollywood faded from the limelight as quickly as they had come. The new star of the year was the American singer, Madonna, whose sultry, sexually-charged singing and style of dress was modelled on Marilyn Monroe. Her big hit in 1985 was *Like a Virgin*.

Popular Films of 1985

Rambo: First Blood, part II, one of a whole crop of violent films glorifying 'American values' – an offshoot of the new US patriotism.

Back to the Future starring Michael J. Fox: aimed at the teenage market but popular with all ages.

The Colour Purple, directed by Steven Spielberg and starring Whoopi Goldberg.

Out of Africa, based on the life of Karen Blixen and starring Meryl Streep and Robert Redford.

My Beautiful Laundrette, written by Hanif Kureishi and directed by Stephen Frears, a study of racial tensions in Britain.

AIDS scare becomes a panic

BY DECEMBER the number of AIDS victims in the USA had risen to over 16,000 – twice as many as in 1984. Over 8000 had already died, including the film star Rock Hudson. Another 100,000 had tested positively for AIDS antibodies in their blood, which meant that they had been in contact with the disease. No one knew how many of them would go on to develop the full-blown syndrome. The number of sufferers in Europe was steadily rising too, and it was predicted that there might be one million cases in Britain by 1991.

Much more was now known about how AIDS spread and how it worked on the immune system. The virus attacked the T-cells, whose job it is to recognize foreign bodies in the bloodstream and eliminate them. Once the T-cells were destroyed, the body could no longer fight off infection, and it was the repeated bouts of infection that eventually led to death. No vaccine or cure was yet in sight. The rapid spread of AIDS was a frightening prospect for individuals and societies. There was some panic among the public, and AIDS victims and homosexuals were sometimes ostracized. The casual and carefree sex of the 1960s and 1970s suddenly seemed dangerous, and sexual habits began to change, especially among gays. AIDS looked like curbing the 'permissive society' in a way that no moral or religious sanctions had ever managed to do. It was feared that by the end of the century medical services everywhere would be stretched beyond breaking point by the strain of caring for millions of chronically-ill people. There was no doubt that AIDS was now an epidemic and that it would be the major health problem of the last part of the twentieth century.

Rock Hudson, one of the 16,000 known AIDS victims in the United States, only months before his death.

Hole found in ozone layer

SCIENTISTS WORKING in the Antarctic discovered that a hole the size of the USA had appeared in the ozone layer of the earth's atmosphere there. Ozone filters the light from the sun and shuts out ultra-violet rays, which can cause skin cancer in humans. The culprits, they believed, were chlorofluorocarbons or CFC 2s, which were used as propellants in aerosols and as fluid in fridges.

No real success with artificial heart

IN NOVEMBER 1984, William Schroeder had become the second man to be fitted with an artificial heart – a more sophisticated version than the one used on Barney Clarke. He lived on, but his life was blighted by a series of strokes that left him partially paralysed. Four more hearts were implanted in 1985 but their recipients all suffered the same sort of complications. De Vries called a halt to the experiments but still thought that the artificial heart would one day have its place as a temporary device to keep seriously-ill patients alive while a suitable human heart was found for transplanting.

Universe running down, say scientists

IN MAY A TEAM OF ASTRONOMERS working in the USA with powerful new radio telescopes, announced that they now had incontrovertible evidence that there was a black hole at the centre of our galaxy. (Black holes are the remnants of dying stars that have collapsed in on themselves and become so dense that their gravity pulls all matter towards them and lets nothing, not even light, escape.) During the course of the year, the same data were gathered for other galaxies as well. This confirmed what scientists had long suspected – that the universe was slowly running down, although the final end would not come for billions of years.

A new generation of computers on the way

JAPAN ANNOUNCED that research was beginning on what was called the 'fifth generation' of computers, with a true artificial intelligence. They would not just think in numbers, as all computers had done up to now, but would be able to use imagination and creative thinking just like a human brain. The actual day when this would happen, though, was still a long way ahead – if it were possible at all.

1986

Disaster at

High radiation levels detected in Scandinavia

IN THE LAST DAYS of April scientists carrying out routine monitoring in Scandinavia detected unusually high levels of radiation in the atmosphere. From the direction the wind was blowing, it seemed to be coming up from the south out of the USSR. The Soviet Union, though, denied that anything unusual had taken place there.

USSR reports 'minor accident'

ON 30 APRIL the Russians admitted that a minor accident had occurred in Number 4 reactor at the Chernobyl nuclear power station in the Ukraine. It was nothing too serious. In the big city of Kiev, 50 miles away, life was going on as normal. Soviet television showed pictures of children playing in its streets. One clue that all was far from well, though, came when the Russians asked for help from abroad in fighting the fire.

Last night the Soviet government issued a statement through Tass (the official Soviet news agency), saying two people had been killed and that evacuation had taken place from the immediate vicinity. The radiation situation at the plant had been stabilised and there was no further cause for concern.
The Times, 30 April

The devastated Number 4 reactor at Chernobyl (marked by the arrow).

USSR admits the truth

MEANWHILE, THE RADIATION CLOUD was spreading across Europe as far as Britain and Greece. Worst hit, apart from parts of Scandinavia, was central Europe. In Poland children were given doses of iodine to ward off its effects. News leaked out that thousands of people were now being evacuated from the Kiev area. An American satellite took pictures of the reactor, which showed damage so great that huge amounts of radiation could not have failed to escape. An American specialist in the effects of radiation, Dr Robert Gale, was invited to treat 300 of the sickest victims with bone marrow transplants. On 14 May the Russians came clean. In a TV speech Gorbachev admitted that a major catastrophe had taken place: 299 people had died in the blast and hundreds more were in hospital with severe radiation poisoning. Nearly 135,000 people had been evacuated from a 30-km-wide zone around the plant, which had now been sealed off. The fire had not been put out completely until the 11 May. Work was going ahead to encase the damaged reactor in a giant concrete tomb, so that no more radiation could ever escape. This, Gorbachev told the world, should be a warning to all.

A great misfortune has befallen us – the accident at the Chernobyl nuclear power plant. For the first time ever, we encountered in reality such a sinister force as nuclear energy that has escaped control.
The accident clearly shows us what devastation would follow if nuclear war befalls mankind.
From Gorbachev's 14 May TV broadcast.

This is it – this is what we've been afraid of all these years; a city devoid of all human life because of radiation.
Dr Robert Gale, as he flew over Pripyat, a town 3 km from Chernobyl.

Chernobyl

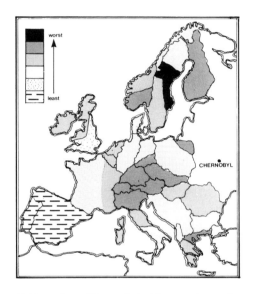

Fall-out from Chernobyl: this map shows the varying intensity of nuclear fall-out over Europe.

The full story is told

AT THE INTERNATIONAL Atomic Energy Agency meeting in Vienna in July, the world heard for the first time exactly what had happened on that disastrous night in April. It was a chilling tale of faulty design and human error. Shortly before midnight on 25 April the staff at the reactor had begun an unauthorized experiment to see how long a generator would continue to produce power when the reactor providing steam for it had been closed down. In their haste they by-passed basic safety procedures. This resulted in an unexpected surge of heat, which turned the water in the reactor (which was supposed to keep the temperature down) into steam and caused an explosion that ruptured the fuel tanks. Only seconds later, as hydrogen and carbon dioxide released in the first explosion came into contact

A cloud over the future

THE CHERNOBYL DISASTER let more radiation out into the environment than all the other nuclear explosions since 1945 put together. The most lethal component of the cloud that passed over Europe was caesium 137, which would pollute the soil for decades and was easily absorbed by human tissue. The area round Chernobyl would not be habitable again in the foreseeable future. The grazing lands of the Lapps in northern Sweden and Finland were so heavily affected that it was likely that thousands of reindeer would have to be slaughtered. Most frightening of all was the threat to health. Most of those who suffered from severe radiation sickness in the immediate aftermath of the blast were now dead or dying. Dr Gale's bone marrow transplants had not been a success. The future health outlook of millions of others all over Europe was uncertain, so too were the genetic effects on those yet unborn. Estimates of future deaths from cancer varied wildly. No one really knew.

with the air, there was a second explosion, throwing a plume of radio-active dust and gas high into the atmosphere. Some of the men at the plant were so terrified that they ran away without even reporting what had happened, although others had shown great courage in staying to fight the fire – at the cost of their own lives. Only the fact that it had happened at night when most local people were indoors and that a strong wind had lofted the dust to a high altitude had kept the casualties around the reactor as low as they were.

Doubts about nuclear power spread

IT WAS NOT JUST what happened at Chernobyl that frightened many people but the fact that it could happen again and again as more and more nuclear power stations were built around the world. A bad accident had already occurred in 1979 at Three Mile Island in the USA. It had been contained in time but only just. Such fears were not helped by widespread doubts about the honesty of most governments, for not only the USSR had lied about the disaster at first. Both the French and British governments had played down the health threat: the French had denied for a week that any radiation had even passed over France, and Britain was slow to ban the sale of sheep from the contaminated areas. The idea that the dream of cheap nuclear energy was just not worth the risks became more widespread, although most governments still went ahead with their building programmes.

Survey of public opinion on nuclear energy		
	Dec 1985	Dec 1986
Percentage of people against building more reactors		
Britain	65	83
USA	67	78
West Germany	46	69
Canada	60	70
Finland	33	64
Survey carried out by Worldwatch Institute, Washington DC		

Americans bomb Tripoli

AFTER THE ATTACKS on Americans abroad in 1985, feelings in the USA were running high, especially against Libya. In the early hours of 15 April US planes, some flying from bases in Britain, bombed the Libyan cities of Tripoli and Benghazi in revenge. Although the targets – according to the Americans – were terrorist training camps, residential areas were hit as well. Most Americans were delighted that their country had struck back at last, but public opinion elsewhere was outraged. In Britain there were demonstrations in protest against the use of British bases. Although Gadaffi vowed revenge against any American abroad, by the end of the year the number of terrorist attacks on them had in fact dropped dramatically.

New wind blows through the Soviet Union

AT THE 27TH PARTY CONGRESS held in February Gorbachev made his most vigorous attack yet on the corruption and stagnation of the Brezhnev years. The Soviet Union would not be a superpower for much longer, he warned, unless great changes were made. For too long the centralized economic system had sheltered inefficient managers and lazy workers, and people at all levels must learn new ways of doing things. Gorbachev called this perestroika or reconstruction. It would only work, though, if everyone, including the Party itself, was honest about what had gone wrong and not afraid to say so. This was glasnost or

Summit meeting ends in bad feeling

REAGAN AND GORBACHEV met again in Reykjavik, Iceland, in October, where Gorbachev presented a sweeping plan to do away with all nuclear weapons by the end of the century so long as the USA also gave up SDI. In a rush of enthusiasm, Reagan almost accepted but then drew back at the prospect of losing Star Wars. There was deadlock, and the summit broke up with nothing agreed, no future meetings planned and a definite chill in the air. However, the talks in Geneva went on.

openness. He called the everlasting war in Afghanistan a 'bleeding wound' that must be staunched as soon as possible.

Marcos ousted

ELECTIONS FOR PRESIDENT were held in the Philippines in February. Using blatant corruption, Marcos just scraped a win against Corazon Aquino. He was now so unpopular, though, that anger on the streets forced him to flee the country only hours after his inauguration. Even the USA, which had a long history of keeping pro-American dictators in power no matter how they behaved, told him to go. Mrs Aquino took over. In the Marcos' former apartments were found a fortune in clothes, shoes and jewels amassed by Imelda Marcos. President Aquino promised a new start with a return to democracy, a release of political detainees and land reform. She faced enormous problems, though, including pro-Marcos officers still in the army, Communist guerillas in the countryside – and her own inexperience. Behind all the rejoicing, the Philippines faced an uncertain future.

Corazon Aquino acknowledges her historic victory over ex-President Marcos.

Oliver North, who acted illegally under his own authority in the Irangate scandal, was, ironically, soon to become a symbol of American patriotism.

Change of leadership in Afghanistan

PRESIDENT KARMAL of Afghanistan, who had been put in power by the Russians when they invaded in 1979, was replaced by Major-General Najibullah, Soviet head of the secret police. The war went on.

Westland scandal threatens Thatcher government

IT WAS NOT ONLY THE US GOVERNMENT that was smeared by scandal. In the New Year the simmering row in Britain over the future of Westland helicopters came right out into the open with a blazing row between Defence Secretary Michael Heseltine and Trade and Industry Minister Leon Brittan. On 9 January Heseltine resigned and marched out of a cabinet meeting at 10 Downing Street. Ten days later a private letter criticizing him was leaked to the press. The leak was traced to Brittan, who had – presumably – wanted to discredit his rival. He resigned in disgrace on the 24th. Mrs Thatcher swore she knew nothing of this trail of back-stabbing and double-dealing in her own government, but there were many – even inside her own party – who had their doubts.

Scandal hits Reagan administration

ON 2 NOVEMBER David Jacobsen, an American hostage who had been held in Beirut for 17 months, was released. Soon afterwards, it came to light that this was the result of a secret deal. The USA had sold weapons to Iran in exchange for Iranian pressure on Hezbollah to free some of its captives. In doing this the Americans had broken their own arms embargo on Iran and their stand against doing deals with terrorists. Even worse, some of the money made from the sales had been sent to the Contras in Nicaragua, thus by-passing Congress's ban on military aid there.

Reagan swore he had known nothing of this shady deal and that it had been masterminded by Lieutenant-Colonel Oliver North, a member of his national security staff, who had exceeded his authority. He set up a committee of inquiry, so too did Congress. At the close of the year, though, the web of accusation and counter accusation was far from being unravelled.

Reagan's popularity sank overnight. By December, many Americans believed that the man who had been respected for his decency and honesty knew more about what had gone on than he was admitting and was busy covering up. Remembering the Watergate scandal that had brought President Nixon down, the press dubbed the scandal 'Irangate' or 'Contragate'.

Commonwealth at loggerheads over sanctions

AT THE COMMONWEALTH CONFERENCE held in London in August, there was a blazing row about the best way to fight apartheid in South Africa. The non-white members voted for sweeping economic sanctions, but Mrs Thatcher voted against. She argued that sanctions would hurt poor blacks and thus fall most heavily on those they were trying to help. The non-white members were so angry that they boycotted the Commonwealth Games held in Edinburgh that summer in retaliation. The Games were a financial disaster.

Enterprise economy on its way

BIG STEPS WERE TAKEN towards the Tory dream of an enterprise economy. British Gas was privatized in November, and four million people bought shares. They soon rose in value so much that many buyers sold at a considerable profit. Personal taxes were cut in the budget, and there were promises of more to come. In October the stock exchange was deregulated. Many of the old curbs on who could deal on stocks and shares and how were swept away. This was dubbed the 'Big Bang'.

The stock market boomed. Overall, the value of shares rose 16 per cent over the year. For those who were already doing well, 1986 was a good year.

Book sales falling

IN BRITAIN and the USA book sales fell throughout the 1980s. The exception was a handful of much-publicized best-sellers in paperback, which sometimes broke all sales records. In Britain pressure from the EEC to put VAT on books and magazines brought protests from writers and publishers, and the idea was shelved.

Bestsellers

France and West Germany:
Parfum (Perfume) – Patrick Susskind
USA:
Love and War, the 2nd volume of a
    civil war saga by John Jakes
Britain:
A Matter of Honour – Jeffrey Archer
Hollywood Wives – Jackie Collins

Government accused of censorship

NORMAN TEBBIT, CHAIRMAN of the Conservative Party, attacked the BBC for what he saw as its biased, anti-American reporting of the Libyan bombing. This was not the first time the BBC had come under fire from the Tories. In 1982 Mrs Thatcher had criticized its handling of the Falklands War. The BBC's retort was that its job was to report the truth as it saw it, not to make propaganda for the government of the day.

The government also tried to prevent the publication in Australia of a book of memoirs by an ex-MI5 agent, Peter Wright, which revealed embarr-assing things about the activities of the secret service. Many people felt that an important principle was at stake here and that the government should not be allowed to curb books or films that told the truth or expressed unorthodox opinions, however embarrassing they might be.

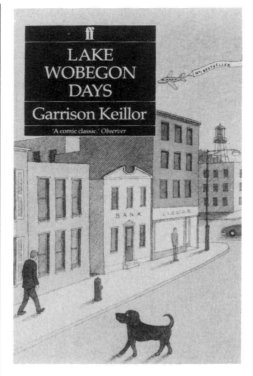

A Bestseller.

New life in Chinese cinema

THE GRADUAL RELAXATION of censor-ship in China since 1976 had led to a spate of interesting films there, which dealt frankly and artistically with subjects that had been forbidden before. Below are some of the best ones to be shown in the West in 1986.

Sacrifice of Youth directed by Chang Luanhsin, a woman director, about the Cultural Revolution.
A Girl of Good Family, about the traumas of an arranged marriage.
Swan Song, which criticized both the excesses of the Cultural Revolution and the consumer society of the 1980s.
Yellow Earth, a graphic picture of peasant-life under Communism.

New novels

The Old Devils – Kingsley Amis
The Handmaid's Tale – Margaret
    Atwood
A Perfect Spy – John le Carré
Lake Wobegon Days – Garrison
    Keillor

Argentina win World Cup

THE WORLD CUP HELD IN MEXICO was won by Argentina, whose captain, Diego Maradona, was the star of the tournament. He caused controversy in the quarter finals against England, though, when he pushed in the first goal with his fist. He told journalists that the ball had been put in the net by 'the hand of God'. After the dour, defensive play of the 1970s, a trend everywhere towards more open, attacking football resulted in entertain-ing games with lots of goals. Gary Lineker of England was the top scorer in the Cup with six.

American sports take off in Britain

AMERICAN FOOTBALL was becoming popular in Britain, and there were now over 100 teams playing it. When 1986 Superbowl champions the Chicago Bears played a game against the Dallas Cowboys at Wembley Stadium in August, 80,000 turned up to watch. One of the stars was the 22 stone (138 kg) William 'Refrigerator' Perry. In the USA itself, though, sport was overshadowed by drug scandals among leading players. Two of them – Len Bias, a basketball star, and Don Rogers of the Cleveland Browns foot-ball team – died from cocaine abuse. The New York Mets won the baseball World Series.

7 die as space shuttle explodes

1986 WAS THE TWENTIETH anniversary of the first manned space flight, and NASA had planned to make it the show-year for its achievements so far. There were 15 space shuttle flights scheduled, but as *Challenger* took off from Cape Canaveral in Florida on 28 January disaster struck. Only 73 seconds after lift-off, it blew up. All seven crew members, including the first civilian in space, Christa McAuliffe, died. It was America's worst-ever space disaster. The cause lay in two tiny rubber rings sealing a joint between two parts of the right-hand rocket booster, which had given way. This had allowed hot exhaust gases to escape and ignite the main fuel tank. Suspicions were voiced that NASA had been so keen to keep to its schedule that it had cut safety corners and had even ignored warnings from its own engineers about minor faults that might have catastrophic effects. It was a great psychological blow to the USA's confidence. All future flights were postponed for at least two years, and it was not clear whether a successor to *Challenger* would ever be built.

The explosion that was seen only a minute after the take off of Challenger.

Channel Tunnel to open in 1993

FRANCE AND BRITAIN finally drew up an agreement to build a railway tunnel – or Chunnel, as it was popularly known – under the English Channel. It was due to open in 1993. Four shuttle trains would carry vehicles and their passengers 40 m below the sea from Cheriton near Folkstone to Frethun near Calais – a trip that would take about 30 minutes. High-speed rail links would also be built from London to the coast and from Calais to Paris, cutting the London-Paris journey time to about three hours. There were inevitable environmental protests in both countries.

Breakthrough in prenatal testing

THE WORK DONE in genetic engineering brought about an important breakthrough in preventing some serious inherited diseases, like Duchenne muscular dystrophy (which usually killed its victims in their teens), cystic fibrosis, thalassaemia and Huntington's Chorea. In these cases a parent could unknowingly carry a defective gene, which did not make them ill but which they passed on to their children, who were affected. In 1985 scientists discovered the gene responsible for muscular dystrophy. Now, using a technique known as 'gene probing', they were able to examine the gene-patterns of parents and unborn children and discover for certain who had inherited the fatal gene and who were carriers. Scientists were confident that they would soon be able to do the same for other genetic defects. At the same time, this new knowledge would involve parents and doctors in some awful personal and ethical decisions.

1987 Change Sweeps

Pace of reform speeds up

GORBACHEV'S CAMPAIGN to restructure Soviet life really took off in 1987. Two major changes were proposed that might alter the face of the Soviet Union for ever. Politics was to be made more democratic by allowing a choice of candidates at elections. Officials would be answerable to the public for what they did, and corrupt or inefficient ones would now be sacked. This was not, nor was it intended to be, democracy in the Western sense. The Communist Party would still remain in overall control and no opposition parties would be allowed.

A house can only be put in order by someone who feels that he owns that house . . . We must increase the degree of democratization in our society . . . one of its main purposes would be to ensure a healthy turnover of officials and raise their level of accountability . . . Activities of the state and public organizations should be more open to scrutiny through the official media and more open to criticism . . . We need democratization to move ahead.
Extracts from Mr Gorbachev's speech to the Party Central Committee, 29 January

Soviet society changing fast

THE FACE OF SOVIET SOCIETY started to change. By the end of the year over 50 private restaurants had sprung up in Moscow, where previously there had been only 83 public eating places for a population of over eight million. People suddenly talked openly in the streets about subjects that had once been taboo. Articles about the seamier side of Soviet life, like crime or drug and alcohol addiction, appeared daily in newspapers and magazines. Even some officials were more frank. The new health minister, Evgeny Chazov, told an interviewer in April that the country's medical services were in a seriously run-down state. Only half the quantity of antibiotics needed was being produced, and some hospitals lacked even basic equipment like scalpels.

Dissidents were released. When Mrs Thatcher visited the USSR at the end of March she was able to break new ground by appearing on live TV to answer questions from three Soviet journalists.

Gorbachev – superstar

STAR OF THE NEW USSR was Party Leader Gorbachev himself, who was highly visible, both at home and abroad, in a way no Soviet leader had been before. Night after night he appeared on TV to drive home the message that perestroika was and must be irreversible. 'We cannot retreat', he told his audience one night, 'for there is nowhere to retreat to'. His wife Raisa, who accompanied him everywhere, had become an important political figure in her own right. She was admired by many as a model of what an emancipated Soviet woman should be like, but her extravagant taste in clothes and jewellery also caused envy and criticism.

Opposition builds up

THERE WAS BOUND to be opposition to the changes from old-time Party members, who distrusted any break with the past. Until August, though, everything seemed to be going Gorbachev's way. Then while he was on holiday in the Caucasus, his critics struck back. The first sign was an article in Pravda by deputy Party Leader, Egor Ligachev, complaining that glasnost had gone too far and was being used by some to undermine the whole fabric of Soviet life. Then on 31 October Boris Yeltsin, the outspoken Moscow Party chief who had been complaining that the pace of reform was too slow, was sacked. The exact circumstances of his dismissal were murky, but it was seen as a victory for the opponents of glasnost.

Economy to be overhauled

THE CENTRALIZED ECONOMIC SYSTEM was also to be overhauled. Factories would now be expected to pay their way and make a profit. Neither workers nor managers could expect a bonus unless the goods they produced were up to scratch. The Co-operative Law, scheduled to come in operation in May, even introduced a shot of private enterprise into the system, making it legal to run 29 categories of private businesses part-time, including taxi-driving, hairdressing, house and car repairs, dressmaking and public catering. Its aim was to make up for the shortfall in consumer goods and services that made daily life in the USSR so difficult.

the Soviet Union

The First Lady: Raisa Gorbachev, seen attending a function with her husband, symbolized glasnost with her glamorous Western style of dress.

Gorbachev strikes back

GORBACHEV STRUCK BACK QUICKLY. The 7 November was the 70th anniversary of the Communist revolution in 1917. Speeches on these occasions are usually full of clichés, but this year Gorbachev's was memorable. He admitted frankly that there was strong resistance to reform in the Party. He then turned to what he called the 'black holes' in Soviet history, like the purges and forcible collectivization of 1932-3 in which millions had died. Up till now historians had been forced either to ignore these events or to lie about them. Now the time had come to review the past with honesty and face up to the mistakes and cruelty that had been done in the name of socialism.

It would be a mistake to take no notice of a certain increase in the resistance of the conservative forces that see perestroika simply as a threat to their selfish interests. This resistance can be felt not only at management levels but also in work collectives . . .

We should learn to spot, expose and neutralize the manoeuvres of the opponents of perestroika, those who act to impede our advance and trip us up, who gloat over our difficulties and setbacks, who try to drag us back.

Part of Gorbachev's speech on the 70th anniversary of the revolution, 7 November

Gorbachev on top but doubts remain

AT THE END of the year Gorbachev was still in charge, but dreams of a new start for the USSR were balanced on a knife edge. He had outmanouevred his opponents, but they were far from cowed. Moreover, unless economic reform led to a rapid rise in living standards, it was only too likely that the enthusiasm of ordinary people for perestroika would wane. So far the omens were not good. The harvest had been only average, and the queues for everyday goods were still long. It was,

Gorbachev himself admitted, far more difficult than he had ever imagined to change the entrenched working habits of a generation. And no one knew what unforeseen consequences glasnost would have. If the relaxation of the police state led to outright rebellion or demands for independence from one of the USSR's many ethnic groups, then a conservative backlash might follow that would sweep Mikhail Gorbachev from power.

INF Treaty signed

ONLY A YEAR after the disappointing end to the 1986 Reykjavik Summit, the superpowers agreed for the first time ever to reduce their stockpiles of nuclear weapons. By the Intermediate Nuclear Forces (INF) Treaty, signed in December, a whole category of missiles – land-based short-and medium-range ones stationed in Europe – was to be dismantled and their bases thrown open to inspection by the other side. Although these weapons made up only about 5 per cent of the world's total nuclear arsenal, it was still a major breakthrough. Gorbachev, who had made it all possible by dropping his insistence on the USA cancelling Star Wars first, went to Washington in person to sign the treaty and was a big hit with the American people. The omens for the START talks (Strategic Arms Reduction Talks) still going on in Geneva to reduce long-range nuclear weapons by 50 per cent suddenly seemed good.

INF is a major event in world politics and a victory for the new political thinking . . . first step towards the actual liquidation of the nuclear arsenal.
Mikhail Gorbachev in his TV address to the Soviet people, 12 December

USA's allies have their doubts

SOME OF THE USA'S ALLIES especially Britain were not so happy about the INF Treaty. The Warsaw Pact was far stronger than NATO in conventional weapons like tanks and aircraft. Now that there were no longer American nuclear weapons stationed in Europe, there would be nothing to deter the Russians from attacking them. They feared that the Americans had been lulled by Gorbachev's charm into believing that the danger from the USSR was past, when they were far from sure that it really was.

'Black Monday': market makers watch their screens anxiously as the previous Friday's collapse on Wall Street begins to hit the London stock market.

Reagan in trouble

AT THE BEGINNING of the year Reagan was in deep trouble at home. A Congressional investigation into Irangate exonerated him from lying but was highly critical of his failure to supervise properly what members of his own staff like Colonel North were up to. Reagan's attempts to defend himself only made him appear old and bumbling. But Reagan's luck held. The Democratic front-runner for the Presidential election next year Gary Hart, a married man, withdrew in May after press reports that he had spent a night aboard a yacht in the Caribbean with a glamorous model, Donna Rice. Then came the INF Treaty and the successful Washington Summit. As 1987 moved into 1988, Reagan's popularity was on the way up again.

US involvement in Gulf stepped up

THE DANGER TO OIL TANKERS using the Gulf and the Straits of Hormuz increased, as Iran stepped up her strategy of mining the waterways. In May the USA announced that in future her navy would protect Kuwaiti ships sailing down the Gulf, as well as her own. That summer and autumn saw some tense incidents. Two Kuwaiti tankers flying the American flag struck mines. On 21 September an Iranian ship, the *Iran Ajr*, was boarded by American commandos as it laid mines in the night. The possibility of a full-scale clash between Iran and the USA seemed very real.

Share prices plummet

SHARE PRICES, to many a symbol of the success of the enterprise culture in the West, had gone on rising throughout the first half of 1987. Then the bubble burst. On 19 October – soon dubbed 'Black Monday' – share prices on Wall Street tumbled by over a quarter in one day, followed by similar collapses throughout the world. The whole international financial system looked on the edge of a total breakdown – awakening memories of the great Crash of 1929 and the depression that followed. In the end, the results were not so disastrous. Few people went bankrupt and the boom went on.

IRA strike in Enniskillen

AFTER A QUIET YEAR so far in Northern Ireland, the IRA set off a bomb during a Remembrance Day ceremony in Enniskillen on 8 November; 11 people died.

Waite disappears in Lebanon

THERE WERE 27 FOREIGNERS now missing in the Lebanon, including nine Americans. In January, Terry Waite, on a mission to free them, disappeared himself. There was still no news of his fate by the end of the year.

Cross-Channel ferry sinks

ON 6 MARCH, the cross-channel car ferry, *Herald of Free Enterprise*, capsized outside Zeebrugge harbour; 190 passengers and crew died. An enquiry blamed three crew members who had failed to close the bow doors properly, but many believed that the real culprits were the owners, Townsend Thoresen, who were trying to run the ferry on the cheap.

The hull of the Herald of Free Enterprise.

Tories win again

IN JUNE THE TORIES won their third election victory in a row, a twentieth-century record. The majority was even larger than last time: 375 seats to Labour's 229. The Alliance failed again, winning only 22 seats. The great divide in voting patterns between Scotland and North England and the prosperous South was even more marked than in 1983. Mrs Thatcher promised that the 'Tory revolution' would go on, for this victory was only 'a staging post on a much longer journey'.

This third defeat in a row was the cause of great soul-searching in the Labour Party. Neil Kinnock told them that it was time to face up to the realities of the new Britain. There was no longer such a thing as a 'natural' Labour voter. Instead the Party must reach out to the 'home-owning, credit-card carrying majority'. Maybe even unilateral disarmament was no longer relevant now that the superpowers were working together to reduce nuclear arsenals. The red flag, symbol of revolution, was replaced by a red rose as the Party's emblem. The left-wing of the Party scorned this as 'designer socialism' (after the current fashion for expensive, designer-label clothes). Whether Kinnock was right remained to be seen.

Alliance break up

AFTER ITS FAILURE to make a spectacular breakthrough, the Alliance fell apart. So too did the SDP itself. Some of its MPs chose to stay with the Liberals, while a smaller number, led by David Owen, broke away to reform the SDP. It had only three MPs in the Commons. The dream of a new alternative to the Labour Party was all but dead. Many people thought it a tragedy that so capable a politician as Owen, who had once been Foreign Secretary, should now be in the political wilderness.

Cultural revolution in the USSR

FOR MANY YEARS Soviet culture of all types had been strictly censored to present only a rosy view of Soviet life. Anything that dealt with the seamier side, past or present, was usually banned. So too were Western influences like rock music or abstract art. Under glasnost all this was changing, and 1987 saw a flood of unorthodox plays and films, some of which had been written many years before but never shown. The USSR's first exhibition of abstract art was held in Moscow in January.

Some first-time Publications in Soviet Culture 1987

Requiem by Anna Akhmatova, a poetic lament to Stalin's victims, written between 1937 and 1940
Children of the Arbat by Anatoly Rybukov, a novel about life in Stalin's Russia.
Repentance directed by Tenghiz Abuladze, a film set in the 1930s
Messenger Boy, a film about young drop-outs in Moscow
Rabbits and Boa Constrictors by Fazil Iksander, a satire of modern Soviet life
Is it Easy to be Young?, a TV documentary series recording the views of young people
Sarcophagus, a play by Vladimir Gubaryev about Chernobyl

English cricket still in trouble

THE POOR RUN by England's cricket team continued. They lost both the summer and winter test series to a brilliant Pakistan side captained by Imran Khan. The winter tour was soured when England captain Mike Gatting and umpire Shakoor Rana quarrelled publicly on the field and brought the game to a halt for over a day. The star of this series was bowler Abdul Qadir, who took 30 wickets in 3 matches.

League gets new sponsor

BARCLAY'S BANK became the new sponsor of the English Football League at the start of the 1987 season. It was now called the Barclays League.

Boxing gets a new champion

SINCE THE EARLY 1980S there had been no single undisputed world heavyweight boxing champion. Rival bodies like the World Boxing Council (WBC) and the World Boxing Association (WBA) had each put up their own claimants. In 1986 American Mike Tyson had beaten the WBC champion Trevor Berbick. Now in 1987 he knocked out the WBA's James 'Bone-crusher' Smith and Tyrell Biggs to become the first undisputed champion for many years – and at only 21 the youngest man ever to hold the title. He had won all 32 of his professional fights.

Mike Tyson overcomes Tony Tucker to become the undisputed world heavyweight champion – and with his exceptional power it seemed unlikely that he would be deposed from this throne for some years to come.

Important breakthrough in physics

PHYSICISTS HAD KNOWN for a long time that when some metals are cooled to absolute zero (-273°C) they lose all resistance to electricity and will conduct a current for ever without it losing any power. This was called super-conductivity. The knowledge was not very usable, though, because the only way to get such a low temperature was with liquid helium, which was very expensive. Then in 1987 scientists succeeded in making a new material able to super-conduct an electrical current at temperatures as high as -173°C, which could be done with cheap liquid nitrogen. The new conductor was a ceramic made from the oxides of yttrium, barium and copper. The possible applications – still only at the drawing-board stage – were exciting and widespread. They included magnetically-levitated high-speed trains, cheaper brain and body scanners, super-high-speed computers and super-conducting electricity cables, which would make sure that next to none of the power generated at power stations was lost on its way to the consumer (at present, over half was lost along the way).

Heatwave causes deaths in Greek islands

GREECE WAS THE LATEST country to be affected by extreme weather conditions. In July, the Greek government declared a state of emergency as the death toll from a national heatwave rose to over 700.

Astronomers see supernova 'close up'

FOR THE FIRST TIME since the arrival of modern technology astronomers were able to view a supernova 'close up' – only thousands and not millions of light years away! Up to now what was known about them was mostly guesswork. On the 24 February the super-giant star Sanduleak in the Magellanic cloud on the edge of our own Milky Way began to shine with a brightness 100 billion times that of the sun. It could be seen clearly with the naked eye from the southern hemisphere for several months before it faded. It also gave off neutrinos – one of the basic particles that make up the matter of the universe. The accumulated evidence confirmed what astronomers already suspected – that a supernova was the death throes of a massive star, whose core had collapsed. The collapse let out all the energy penned up in the core, causing a giant shock wave.

British research under threat

IN BRITAIN THE FUTURE of scientific research was being threatened by cutbacks in government spending. Most grants were now given only for specific projects that had a clear practical end in view, like the Centre for Superconductivity in Cambridge. Funds for fundamental theoretical research, which might or might not lead anywhere, were now given to only a small number of universities. Scientists argued that these were false economies that misunderstood what science was all about. Many of the key discoveries in the past like penicillin had been made quite accidentally by scientists who were looking for something else.

Africa in grip of AIDS epidemic

THE WORLD HEALTH ORGANIZATION reported that Central Africa was in the grip of an AIDS epidemic far more widespread than that in the West. All types of people were affected, heterosexuals as much as gays. Many babies were being born who had been infected from their mothers in the womb. In Zaire, for example, 8 per cent of women who gave birth in hospital carried the disease. Doctors now believed that AIDS in fact originated in Africa, possibly from the bites of infected monkeys, and spread by chance into the gay population of the USA.

Nations get together to save ozone layer

DELEGATES FROM 70 nations met in Montreal in September and drew up an agreement to cut their use of CFC 2s in half by 1999.

Man-made rain tames forest fire

THE WORST FIRE in Communist China's history was put out by nearly half an inch of artificial rain. The fire, which was in the Doxinganlikng Forest in north-east China, threatened to spread across the border with the Soviet Union. After fire-fighters had battled against the two remaining areas of fire, the authorities resorted to artificial rain. More than 3000 shells of silver iodide were fired into the air and dry ice was spread in the sky to create the rain. The operation was a success.

1988

An End to the

40 years of tension

FOR OVER 40 YEARS the Cold War had threatened the peace of the world and turned every quarrel from Berlin to south-east Asia into a potential nuclear confrontation that could bring all human life to an end. No thaw ever lasted long or changed anything for good. Since 1985 tensions between the superpowers had eased again but how long it would last this time no one knew.

USSR set to leave Afghanistan

ON 14 APRIL the Soviets agreed to take troops out of Afghanistan by 15 February 1989. This was something quite unprecedented – the first time the Russians had agreed to withdraw from a country they had taken over and the first real breach in the Brezhnev Doctrine. Even sceptics on the West did not doubt they meant what they said and that the Russians had at last accepted the bitter truth that this was a war they could never win. After nine years, the deaths of 13,000 Soviets and over one million Afghans, four million refugees and a country in ruins, all they would leave behind was the tottering government of President Najibullah, whom no one believed would last long once the Red Army had gone. The situation was not very different from the one they had come to rescue, just like the Americans in Vietnam before them.

The end: Soviet troops withdraw from Afghanistan.

Talks begin over Angola

IN MAY TALKS BEGAN at last to find a settlement to the thorny Angolan problem. Although it was the Cubans

Russian troops go home

ON 14 AUGUST RADIO MOSCOW announced that half the Soviet troops stationed in Afghanistan had already left – ahead of the timetable agreed on in April. No one doubted they were telling the truth.

and South Africans rather than the superpowers themselves who had intervened in the civil war there since 1975, it had long been clear that both the USA and USSR were pulling the strings behind the scenes. If they could agree not to use Angola as a Cold War battleground anymore, then there was a chance that the Cubans and South Africans and the warring factions inside Angola itself might be forced to make peace. In November a timetable for Cuban and South African withdrawal was finally drawn up. Many observers saw the hand of President Gorbachev behind the deal.

Cold War

Reagan and Gorbachev meet again

AT THE BEGINNING OF JUNE Reagan and Gorbachev held their fourth summit – this time in Moscow – but hopes that it might be the occasion for the signing of a ground-breaking START treaty were dashed. The meeting broke up in some ill-feeling when Reagan publicly criticized the Soviet Union's human rights record and invited three prominent dissidents to the American embassy, provoking an angry outburst from Gorbachev. Nonetheless, there was no breakdown this time. Both leaders agreed that East-West dialogue must go on and that Reagan's retirement in the coming November must not be allowed to interrupt it. The future of the world depended on it.

Our dialogue has not been easy but we mustered enough political realism and will to overcome barriers and divert from the way of dangerous confrontation. Though it goes much more slowly than is demanded by the situation . . . I have understood, Mr President, that you are willing to continue our joint endeavours. For my part, I can assure you that we will do everything in our power to move much more rapidly.
From Mr Gorbachev's farewell speech to President Reagan, Moscow, 2 June

Smiles all round: the relaxed relationship between the two leaders, Reagan and Gorbachev, contributed to the new era in superpower relations.

East-West barriers come down

IN THE SUMMER OF 1988 the world saw some amazing sights. In July the Soviet Chief of Staff, Marshal Sergei Akhromeyev, arrived in the USA on a six-day tour. During his trip, he sat at the controls of a B-1 bomber and held a press conference in the Pentagon, the hub of the US military machine. Soviet officers visited Greenham Common and inspected the empty sheds where the missiles, now gone, used to be stored. The women's camp too had gone – it was needed no longer.

A speech that shook the world

THE CLIMAX OF THE YEAR came at the United Nations in December, when President Gorbachev unveiled his vision of the future. A world facing nuclear annihilation, environmental pollution and terrible poverty over two-thirds of the globe could, he argued, no longer afford the Cold War. Instead, everyone must work together to bring peace to the world's hot-spots and pool their resources to end poverty and rescue the environment. Among his concrete suggestions were a 100-year moratorium on interest payments by the poorest nations and a UN-backed peace corps to rebuild Afghanistan. The USSR herself would take the first step towards disarmament by cutting its armed forces by 500,000 men, including 50,000 troops, 10,000 tanks and 88 aircraft now stationed in Eastern Europe and nearly all those on the Chinese frontier. This, he hoped, would inspire NATO to do the same and be only a beginning.

No one had heard, or ever expected to hear, such a speech from a Soviet leader before. Delegates from 159 nations stood up to applaud him as he finished. To many it seemed as if an end to the Cold War was in sight at last.

It would be a mistake to think that the problems plaguing mankind today can be solved with means and methods which were applied or seemed to work in the past . . . today we face a different world for which we must seek a different road to the future . . . it is obvious, for example, that the use or threat of force can no longer and must no longer be an instrument of foreign policy. This applies, above all, to nuclear arms. But that is not the only thing that matters. All of us, and primarily the stronger of us, must exercise self-restraint and totally rule out any use of force.
President Gorbachev to the United Nations General Assembly, 7 December

Gorbachev keeps control but perestroika in trouble

RUMOURS CONTINUED throughout the year about the challenge Mr Gorbachev faced from conservatives within the Party, but he held his own. In October he removed the elderly president Gromyko, took over as President himself and demoted long-time critic, Egor Ligachev. The 29th Party Congress held in July, which was televised, was remarkable for its outspoken speeches that he allowed from the floor. Perestroika itself was struggling, though. When Gorbachev went on a walkabout in Krasnoyarsk in September, he was mobbed by angry citizens complaining that housing and food shortages were as bad as ever. This was seen on TV all over the USSR.

Nationalist tensions flare in USSR

THE FEAR THAT GLASNOST might trigger off ethnic tensions that would tear the USSR apart seemed to come a step nearer. In February an old quarrel between the southern republics of Armenia and Azerbaijan flared up into outright violence. In the town of Sumgait 31 people died and troops had to be sent in to quieten things down. The tension lasted all year and was no nearer a solution at the end. Huge popular demonstrations were held in the Baltic States of Latvia, Lithuania and Estonia in favour of greater freedom from Moscow. A showdown was avoided this time but who knew what would happen if things really got out of hand or the nationalist bug spread to other republics – the very existence of the USSR itself would be at stake.

Ceasefire in Gulf

THE GULF WAR was going badly for Iran. In April she suffered a crushing defeat on land. A week later, clashes with US warships destroyed most of her navy on a single day. Her economy was in a shambles. Then on 3 July one of her civil airliners was shot down over the Gulf from a US cruiser, the *Vincennes*, killing all 290 on board. The captain of the *Vincennes* claimed that it had been mistaken for an enemy war plane. On 24 July Iran asked for a ceasefire and one of the twentieth century's longest wars came to an end – and with it Khomeini's dream of spreading his brand of Islam across the Middle East.

Making this decision was more deadly than taking poison. I submit myself to God's will and drink this draught for his satisfaction.
From Ayatollah Khomeini's broadcast to the Iranian people, 20 July

Running for President: George Bush and his campaign staff jogging through Chicago on the election trail.

Britain is back – but with reservations

BY THE LATE 1980S Britain had the fastest growing economy in Europe. A number of surveys carried out that year, however, indicated that many Britons were worried that important human values had been lost in the rush to get rich. The enterprise culture and consumer society encouraged selfishness and debt. Violence and drunkenness were on the rise, so too was boorish behaviour, which had nothing to with poverty or deprivation. It was fashionable among some affluent young men – the so-called lager louts – to drink too much and go on the rampage. Lower taxes made individuals richer but led to a decline in the standard of public services. While sales of consumer goods boomed, the sewers beneath Britain's cities were decaying and were not being repaired. The National Health service was short of funds. Waiting lists were long, and some patients, including babies with heart defects, died while waiting for operations. Morale among NHS staff was low. Some nurses even went on strike – the first time this had ever happened. Accidents, like the Zeebrugge and Clapham ones, were on the increase – caused, maybe, by employers cutting safety corners in the scramble for profits. Many people were worried about what would happen when water and electricity were privatized the following year.

USA gets a new President

1988 WAS ELECTION YEAR in the USA. Riding high on Reagan's popularity, Vice-President George Bush won a clear victory over Democrat Michael Dukakis, even though Bush's name was smeared with Irangate. He also chose a weak running-mate, Senator Dan Quayle, who was rumoured to have bought his way out of the draft during the Vietnam War. Democrats, though, won control of both houses of Congress.

Anglo-Irish agreement fails

THE ANGLO-IRISH AGREEMENT of 1985 flopped when a Dublin court refused to extradite Father Patrick Ryan, who was wanted in Britain on terrorist charges. There was little faith left in the agreement in England now, and a solution to the troubles of Northern Ireland seemed as far away as ever.

Year ends in tragedy

WHAT MANY PEOPLE would remember most about 1988, though, were the string of disasters – natural and man-made – that marked its closing months. Greatest loss of life was in the earthquake that hit Soviet Armenia on 7 December, all but wiping out three large towns. An estimated 50,000 died and hundreds of thousands more made homeless. It would take years to rebuild the shattered lives and towns. Four days before Christmas a Pan Am Boeing en route from London to New York exploded in the air over the Scottish town of Lockerbie. All on the plane died, so did 11 people on the ground. A bomb was blamed, but who had planted it no one really knew. Feelings ran high as news leaked out that Pan Am had had warning in advance that one of their flights might be sabotaged but had not warned passengers. In the same month, 36 people died at Clapham Junction in Britain's worst train crash for 20 years.

THE TOWN OF SPITAK DOES NOT EXIST ANY MORE.
Headline in *Pravda*, 9 December

Woman to lead Muslim nation

IN NOVEMBER BENAZIR BHUTTO became Prime Minister of Pakistan, the first woman to head a modern Muslim state.

New Party formed

THE LIBERAL PARTY and some members of the old SDP joined together to form a new party, the Social and Liberal Democrats, to be known as the Democrats. David Steel resigned and Paddy Ashdown was voted the new leader.

Scandal in the food industry

IN DECEMBER Junior Health Minister, Edwina Currie, told the press that most of the eggs produced in Britain were infected with salmonella, which could cause serious food poisoning. Sales of eggs dropped dramatically. The powerful farming lobby was so angry that she was sacked, but this did not kill the suspicion that she might be right.

How has Britain changed over the past 10 years	
	%
Richer	48
Poorer	36
More freedom	44
Less freedom	24
Less happy	48
More happy	21
More selfish	61
More generous	19

Observer/Harris Poll on people's feelings about what had happened to the British people in the nine years since Mrs Thatcher took over, published in the *Observer*, 22 May

Sport and the Arts

New cult of peace, love and music

THE 'IN' MUSICAL CULT in Britain was Acid House. It was not just a sound but a whole way of relaxation and fun, based on the hallucinatory drug Ecstasy. Fans gathered together in clubs to take drugs and dance to recorded electronic music with a heavy background beat, a follow-on the hip-hop and house music of the first half of the decade. The first of the clubs and the one on which the others were modelled was the Shoom Club in London. The mood was usually playful, non-violent and spontaneous, reminiscent in some ways of the peace and love cult of the 1960s. Some saw it as a reaction against the selfish, 'me first' mood of Thatcher's Britain, but many adults were shocked by the wide-spread use of drugs.

Shoomers is just like one big happy family, who care about each other. Everyone is a totally different character, but special in their own way.
Extract from the Shoomers' booklet.

The spirit of peace and love captured on an 'acid house' record cover.

Rock stars sing for Mandela

THE IDEALISTIC MOOD of rock music went on. A crowd of 70,000 gathered at Wembley Stadium on 11 June to listen to an all-day concert to mark the 70th birthday of imprisoned South African nationalist Nelson Mandela. The main spirit behind it was Jerry Dammers of The Specials. The performers included not only well-known stars like Stevie Wonder, Chubby Checker, Simple Minds and UB40, but also singers and bands from Third World countries who had never played in the West before.

New Films and Plays
Fatal Attraction, where love turned sour
The Last Emperor, a spectacular epic directed by Bernardo Bertolucci; it won nine Oscars
Bird, a personal tribute to the jazz musician Charlie Parker, directed by Clint Eastwood
Who Framed Roger Rabbit?, a clever mixture of real actors and cartoon characters that triggered off a whole new 'rabbitmania' industry in the USA
The Last Temptation of Christ, directed by Martin Scorsese, which caused outrage among many Christians
Perdition was finally staged at the Royal Court in London

Australian soap a big hit

THE BRITISH PASSION for soap operas went on. The most popular programme on TV this year was the Australian soap *Neighbours*, which drew an audience of nearly 20 million daily.

Martina's reign ends

MARTINA NAVRATILOVA'S reign as the queen of world tennis ended when 18-year-old Steffi Graf from West Germany achieved the Grand Slam by winning all four major tournaments, including Wimbledon.

Drug scandals sour Olympics

THE OLYMPIC GAMES held in Seoul, South Korea – the first with all the big nations there since 1976 – were over-shadowed by a major drugs scandal. Canadian runner Ben Johnson, who broke the world record in the 100 m, was stripped of his gold medal and sent home in disgrace after traces of illegal steroids were found in his bloodstream. The most remarkable performance was by Florence Griffith-Joyner of the USA. She won the 100 m and 200 m in times that would have beaten the men in the 1952 Games. The old generation of athletes, including Daley Thompson, Ed Moses and Steve Cram, faded. Coe and Ovett did not even compete.

Ben Johnson signals '1' to the crowds in the Seoul Olympic stadium after he recorded the fastest ever time run over 100 metres.

Damage being done to earth's atmosphere now beyond doubt

THIS WAS THE YEAR in which any lingering doubts about the damage man was doing to the atmosphere around him were swept away. The global temperature in the first five months was 0.22°C warmer than usual and scientists were '99 per cent' convinced that it was due to the greenhouse effect and not just chance. All that they disagreed on now was how much warmer the earth would get between now and the end of the century. Estimates varied between 1-4°C. A new hole in the ozone layer was found above Spitzbergen in the Arctic, and the Antarctic one was already nearly twice as large as it had been in 1985. Far more drastic changes than those in the Montreal Agreement would have to be made if things were not to get worse.

US drought a taste of things to come

IN THE SPRING and summer the USA was struck by the worst drought in over 50 years, wiping out much of the corn and soya crop. Many people believed the worst.

It is a warning. Whether or not it is related to global changes, it provides a small taste of the dislocations society will face with increasing frequency if we fail to act.
Dr James Hansen of NASA on the US drought, reported in *The Guardian*, 25 June

We only have one planet. If we screw it up, we have no place to go.
Senator Bennett Johnson of Louisiana during the debate on the environment in the US Senate, 21-24 June.

Space shuttle flies again

ON 2 OCTOBER, two-and-a-half years after the *Challenger* disaster, the new space shuttle *Discovery* blasted off. $2 billion had been spent modifying the design so that the same disaster would not happen again. The American dream of conquering space would go on. The Russians, too, launched their first shuttle on 15 November. Called *Burin* or *Snowstorm*, one of its main jobs would be to ferry cosmonauts to and from the big space station, *Mir 2*, planned for the mid 1990s as the base for a manned mission to Mars. The Russians had spent much of the 1970s and 1980s quietly preparing for long-distance space travel by carrying out experiments to see how the human body would stand up to long periods in space. In December two cosmonauts, Vladimir Titov and Musa Manarov, came back to earth after spending a record 370 days on board a space station. Europe too put up a rocket – its fourth. Called *Ariane 4*, its job was to put communications satellites into orbit. The European Space Agency was now the world's leading commercial satellite-launching business.

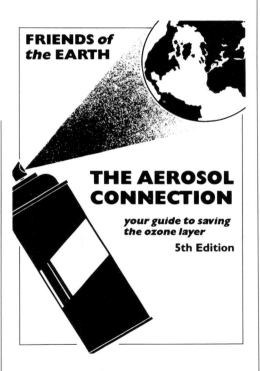

FRIENDS *of* the EARTH

THE AEROSOL CONNECTION

your guide to saving the ozone layer
5th Edition

The Aerosol Connection: *this booklet, published by the Friends of the Earth, included a 26-page-long list of aerosol sprays that would not damage the ozone layer.*

Cell transplants come under fire

IN BRITAIN A NEW and controversial type of transplant was carried out. Cells from the brain of an aborted foetus were injected into the brains of two people suffering from Parkinson's Disease. Parkinson's patients have a deficiency of dopamine, a chemical substance made in the brain, and it was hoped that the transplanted cells would take and grow and start making good the shortage. By the end of the year the omens were good, as both patients had shown some improvement. Similar, less-publicized, work was already being done in isolating the cells in foetuses that made insulin and planting them in diabetics, who, it was hoped, would then start making insulin for themselves, making daily injections unnecessary. As with so many new medical techniques, many people had grave doubts about the moral issues involved. It was feared, for example, that a woman might become pregnant merely to provide a relative with the cells they needed to cure a disease.

1989 Eastern Europe

Infectious spirit of Glasnost

SO FAR THE DRAMATIC CHANGES taking place in the USSR had failed to shake the Soviet-backed dictatorships of Eastern Europe. Only in Hungary, where the Communist Party had sacked its long-time boss, Janos Kadar, in May 1988 and promised a more open political system, had things begun to move. That the spirit of glasnost would be infectious seemed inevitable. That it would happen so fast in 1989 took everyone by surprise.

It was the Hungarians who began this remarkable year of change by being the first to discover that the incredible was true: that dictatorship could be shrugged off without catastrophe, that there were no longer Soviet tanks lurking on the horizon. As the message sank in, it signalled the end of that old East European companion, Comrade Fear.
From a review of 1989 in *The Independent*, 29 December

Poland kicks off

THE FIRST SURPRISE was Poland, where the seven-year ban on Solidarity was lifted in January, and both sides agreed to work together to revive the decaying Polish economy – an open admission by the Communist Party that they could no longer rule alone, without the consent of the people. In June the first free elections since the war were held. Solidarity candidates swept the board, and one of them, Tadeusz Mazowiecki, became Prime Minister. In the past similar revolutions in Eastern Europe had been crushed by Soviet tanks. This time it was different. The Brezhnev Doctrine, Soviet spokesman Gennady Gerasimov told Western reporters, had been replaced by the 'Sinatra Doctrine', allowing the Eastern bloc countries to "do it their way".

And the wall comes tumbling down . . . thousands of people from East and West gather together around the symbol of division of the two parts of their country.

East Germans rebel

FOR DECADES EAST GERMANY had been the strictest, most closed-in of the satellite states. That summer, however, East Germans wanting to escape discovered a gaping hole in the Iron Curtain. Take a holiday in Hungary – one of the few countries they could visit without permission – and walk into Austria. By the end of September, as the news spread, the trickle of refugees had become a flood of over 3000 a day. In October Mr Gorbachev visited East Berlin. Thousands poured onto the streets to greet him. He told hardline leader Erich Honecke that he must adapt to the spirit of the new age or face a popular revolution – and no Soviet tanks would come to bail him out. When Gorbachev flew home, the demonstrations went on. On 9 October tens of thousands took to the streets of Leipzig, chanting 'We are the people'. At an emergency meeting of the ruling Politburo, Honecke voted to send the army in to crush the demonstrators by force. He was over-ruled and resigned. Egon Krenz, who took over, promised reform.

Hungary's borders open

QUIETLY HUNGARY had been moving towards democracy. In October its Communist Party declared itself dissolved. The 1956 uprising, which had been crushed by the Red Army, was openly celebrated, its leaders rehabilitated, the huge red star on top of the parliament building in Budapest torn down. Hungary's border with Western Europe was thrown open.

Breaks Free

The wall opens

THE FIRST REFORM came on the afternoon of Thursday 9 November. In future, it was announced, East Germans would be allowed to travel freely outside the country. That evening a handful of East Berliners tried to cross the Berlin Wall into West Berlin and were waved through by the guards. As the news spread, hundreds of thousands of East and West Berliners flocked to the crossing points and mingled freely together for the first time in nearly 30 years in what journalists dubbed 'Europe's greatest-ever street party'. By the time the weekend was over the barriers had gone, giving rise to talk that Germany might one day be reunited again. A month later Krenz himself was swept aside as demands for change went on. The dreaded secret police, the Stasi, was abolished.

Now we shall all be out of a job
An East Berlin border guard, quoted in *The Independent*, 11 November

I just can't grasp it, it's simply too much for me. To think it should happen in my lifetime.
A middle-aged East Berlin taxi driver, on the night the Berlin wall opened, quoted in *The Independent*, 11 November

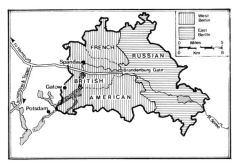

The division of Berlin.

Events move fast in Czechoslovakia

FOR A WHILE, Czechoslovakia, whose own wave of change had been crushed by Soviet tanks in 1968, remained strangely quiet. Then on 17 November students took to the streets of Prague demanding change. The protest was brutally broken up by riot police and the country erupted. Huge demonstrations against the hated Communist Party leadership were held every night in the major cities. Alexander Dubcek, leader of the Prague Spring of 1968 and still a symbol of hope to many, made his first public speech for over 20 years. Within a week the Communist leaders had been forced to resign, a coalition government sworn in and free elections promised for 1990. Vaclav Havel, a playwright and long-time leader of the underground opposition, who only nine months before had been in prison, was sworn in as President on 29 December. Moscow even set its seal of approval on events by apologizing for the invasion of 1968.

Civil War in Romania

PRESIDENT CEAUSESCU of Romania was different from the other East European leaders, for he did not owe his power to Soviet support. If anyone could survive the deluge of change, it would be him. For over 20 years, he and his family, who held nearly all the top jobs, had held the country in a tight grip, backed up by a fanatical secret police force, the Securitate. Then in mid-December the police attempted to arrest a pastor, Laszlo Tokes, a critic of Ceausescu, in the western city of Timisoara. When members of his congregation formed a human chain around the church to protect him, they were shot down. Up to 2000 people, including women and children, died. It was the spark that set Romania alight. Within days a public appearance by Ceausescu in Bucharest had turned into a huge demonstration against him. The army, ordered to break up the protests, backed the people instead. Unnerved, the Ceausescus tried to flee, only to be recognized and captured. After a brief trial, later shown on video, they were shot on Christmas Day.

There was to be no easy victory for the Romanian people, though. Just when it seemed that they had won, the Securitate struck back. For three days civil war raged on the streets of Romania's cities, leaving thousands dead, before the army came out on top. An interim government of Ceausescu's opponents, promised free elections.

As 1989 passed into 1990, only tiny Albania remained untouched by the wind of change sweeping through Eastern Europe.

It was as if the whole city was on the streets. Many of the demonstrators were students and schoolchildren but there were plenty of old people as well . . . Then I heard the sound of firing. But it wasn't the army but the Securitate who were firing. They were shooting from helicopters in the air as well . . . One person saw two dead children being carried away in a white linen cloth. Some people were shouting to us, 'Tell the Yugoslav people what is happening to us.'
Yugoslav witness to events in Timisoara, 18 December, quoted in *The Guardian*

Bloodshed in Peking

IT WAS NOT ONLY IN EUROPE that President Gorbachev's presence caused a stir. In May he paid a visit to China that was intended to bury three decades of hostility between the two nations. No sooner had he arrived than student protests for greater democracy, which had begun several weeks before, intensified. In Peking, thousands occupied Tiananmen Square and were joined everyday by a growing number of ordinary citizens from factory workers to pensioners. It looked as though a popular revolution was in the making.

For weeks the government – split between reformers like Zhao Ziyang who sympathized with the students and hardliners like Deng Xiaoping and Li Peng who wanted to crush them – was paralysed, and China's future hung in the balance. In the end the hardliners came out on top. On 2 June the army was sent in, only to be stopped by human barricades. Some of the soldiers even threw down their weapons and joined the protesters. For a while it looked as though the students had won. In the early hours of Sunday 4 June, however, the government struck again. This time there was no reprieve. Crack army units swept into Peking with their machine guns firing indiscriminately.

No one knows how many died, only that it ran into thousands. The democracy movement was crushed and the slow liberalization of China that had begun after Mao's death in 1976 put into reverse. These events caused great alarm and fear in Hong Kong, which was due to be handed over to China in 1997.

The calm before the storm: students mass around their hastily-erected Statue of Liberty in Tiananmen Square in defiance of the onlooking Mao. Two days later the calm was to be shattered when the People's Army turned on them.

USSR in trouble

WHILE PRESIDENT GORBACHEV was fêted like a hero abroad, his troubles at home multiplied. Inspite of perestroika the economy continued to deteriorate.

Cold War is over – that's official

COLD WAR TENSIONS continued to subside around the world. In January the USSR announced that it was cutting its armed forces by 14 per cent and destroying its chemical weapons stockpiles. The Angolan agreement struck in 1988 held, and the South Africans and Cubans went home. South Africa gave independence to Namibia, exiles like Sam Nujoma returned home and the elections supervised by the United Nations were held in November. As expected, these were won by SWAPO.

In February – dead on schedule – the last Soviet troops left Afghanistan. Against all expectations the Communist government in Kabul survived, for the Mujaheddin guerillas soon fell to quarrelling among themselves. America's new president George Bush and Mikhail Gorbachev held a summit meeting aboard a cruise ship in the Mediterranean in early December. As it ended at 12.45 pm (Maltese time) on 3 December Gennady Gerasimov announced that from that moment onwards the Cold War was officially over.

Shortages of essentials like soap and toothpaste got worse, and the grain harvest fell well below target. Inflation rose to around 10 per cent. In the summer, Siberian miners came out on strike and almost brought the economy to a standstill. Nationalist unrest grew, not only in the Baltic States but in Georgia and Moldavia as well and was bound to grow worse as revolt spread in Eastern Europe. In August two million people linked arms to form a chain 370 miles long through Estonia, Latvia and Lithuania in commemoration of the Soviet annexation of the provinces in 1940. Whether the country could be held together without force remained doubtful. Gorbachev himself came under attack from both ordinary people frustrated by worsening living conditions and party hardliners. He survived – but the future of the USSR hung in the balance.

Tory revolution runs out of steam

IN BRITAIN THE GREAT ECONOMIC BOOM ran into trouble. Rising imports of foreign consumer goods plunged the balance of payments deeply into the red. Inflation rose to nearly 8 per cent. To counteract this, Chancellor Lawson pushed interest rates up, causing problems for millions of mortgage-holders. Repossessions became common and homelessness rose. In October Lawson resigned amidst rumours that he had quarrelled with the Prime Minister. The new community charge or poll tax, planned to replace the rates, was deeply unpopular, as was the proposed privatization of the electricity supply, which had to be postponed. The Tory vote slumped in the Euro-elections, while the Labour Party's popularity rose. It seemed as if the ten-year Tory domination of British politics might be drawing to a close.

Signs of Change in South Africa

THERE WERE STIRRINGS of change in South Africa. In August the despised President Botha resigned and was replaced by R.W. de Klerk. During the year some towns relaxed petty rules over segregated beaches and swimming pools. In October Walter Sisulu of the African National Congress was released from prison, and there were rumours that the release of Nelson Mandela himself might not be far off. Whether these changes would prove to be only cosmetic or the start of much more fundamental political reforms remained to be seen.

Khomeini dies

IN JUNE THE AYATOLLAH KHOMEINI, inspirer of the Islamic revolution that had shaken the world in the 1980s, died in Teheran. His funeral was the occasion for a massive outpouring of grief among Iranians. Hopes that his death would bring an end to his fanatical Islamic republic and release for the hostages in Lebanon proved premature, however.

Guildford Four released

IN 1975 THREE IRISHMEN and one woman had been convicted of planting a bomb that killed servicemen in a pub in Guildford in 1974, although they never stopped protesting their innocence. In October 1989 the Court of Appeal decided that the police evidence that had convicted them had indeed been rigged, and the four were released. The reputation of the British police, which had been falling throughout the 1980s, reached a new low.

Green issues come to the fore

THE ENVIRONMENT became an important political issue in 1989. In the June elections to the European Parliament the ecological vote was up everywhere, especially in Britain, where the Green Party, hitherto a bit of a joke, won 15 per cent of the vote. By the end of the year one-fifth of the 23 million cars on Britain's roads had switched over to lead-free petrol, and there was a rush among manufacturers to market 'environmentally friendly' products, like phosphate-free washing powder. Politicians of all parties now paid lip-service to green issues, but whether this would lead to serious action being taken to save the environment remained to be seen.

Drug wars tear US cities apart

FOR A NUMBER OF YEARS addiction to crack – an inhalable form of cocaine cheap to make and easy to take – had been spreading through the poor neighbourhoods of the inner cities in the USA. By 1989 it had reached epidemic proportions, blighting the lives of hundreds of thousands, especially among the young. Wars between rival drugs gangs had made those cities more dangerous than ever. In Washington, DC, (population 600,000), there were 112 murders in the first two-and-a-half months of the year – more than Britain (population 55 million) had in a whole year.

In an almost farcical footnote to the drugs crisis, the USA tried all year to oust the Panamanian leader, General Noriega, who was suspected of being involved in drug trafficking. On 20 December US troops even invaded and occupied Panama, but failed to capture Noriega, who found asylum in the Vatican embassy in Panama City.

Author faces death threat

THE BIGGEST CULTURAL story of 1989 had more to do with politics than art. *The Satanic Verses* by Salman Rushdie, an Indian by birth who lived in Britain, was an allegorical novel on the modern world. Among the passages in the book, which also satirized Britain and in which Mrs Thatcher appeared as *Mrs Torture*, were disrespectful references to Islam, including a dream sequence in which five prostitutes live out a fantasy that they are the wives of the prophet Mohammed. The book caused an uproar among pious Muslims all over the world and copies of it were burned on the streets of Bradford. The climax came in February when Ayatollah Khomeini issued an order for Rushdie's execution on the grounds of blasphemy, forcing him and his wife into hiding under police protection. The Ayatollah's edict sparked off a major argument among intellectuals all over the world about the rights and limitations of free expression. Did artists have the right to express whatever they liked, however offensive it might be to some, or was it justified to use censorship to protect religious or racial sensibilities?

. . . the author of *The Satanic Verses* . . . and all those involved in its publication who are aware of its content, are sentenced to death.
Ayatollah Khomeini's edict, broadcast on Teheran radio, 14 February

We . . . are distressed and outraged by the Ayatollah Khomeini's call for the murder of Salman Rushdie.
From a protest issued by a group of British writers and journalists, 15 February

Salman Rushdie, who became a focus of Muslim anger when his book The Satanic Verses *was deemed to be blasphemous.*

Cup semi-final leads to tragedy

AT THE FA CUP SEMI-FINAL between Liverpool and Nottingham Forest at Hillsborough, overcrowding on the terraces led to 95 Liverpool fans being crushed to death. The match was abandoned, although Liverpool went on to win the Cup later. UEFA refused to reconsider England's readmission to European competitions until safety standards in stadiums had been improved.

Grand Prix bitter rivalry

THE WORLD FORMULA 1 motor-racing championship ended sourly with accusations of reckless driving against both Britain's Nigel Mansell and Brazil's Ayrton Senna. In the final race, the Australian Grand Prix, which Senna had to win if he was to become champion, his rival Alain Prost accused him of being so desperate to win at all costs that he vetoed an attempt by other drivers to have the race called off because of appalling weather conditions. In the end, only eight out of the 26 cars that started finished. Among the casualties was Senna, who crashed. Prost won the championship.

Hits of the Year
Media Stars of Year – *Neighbours'* stars Kylie Minogue and Jason Donovan, both of whom had several hit records.

Best-selling novel – *Rivals* by Jilly Cooper

Most popular film – *Batman, the Movie*, which made $52 million at the box office in the first six days after its release in the USA.

Best-selling album – *A New Flame* by Simply Red

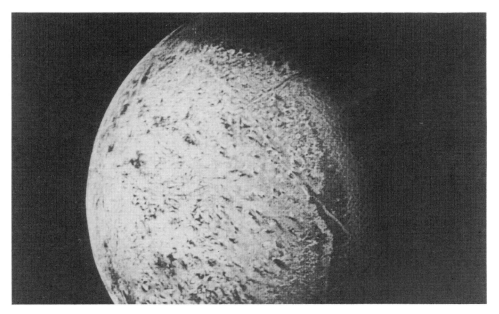

One of the remarkable views of Neptune's moon Triton taken by Voyager II.

Voyager's 12-year tour nearing its end

ONE OF THE EPIC scientific stories of the 1980s had been the flight of the two US *Voyager* spacecraft, launched in 1977, through the solar system. The climax came on 25 August when *Voyager 2* skimmed 3000 miles above the planet Neptune on the outer fringes of the system, three billion miles from earth, and sent back a series of pictures that taught scientists things about the distant planet that could never have been learned through telescopes. The technological obstacles overcome had been astounding. On the outer edge of the solar system, where light levels are 1000 times dimmer than around Earth, the solar cells that are normally used to power spacecraft do not work. *Voyager* had been powered on board by a small atomic generator. After its Neptune fly-past, *Voyager 2*, like its sister-craft years before, headed towards inter-stellar space.

From the data scientists learned that, contrary to expectations, Neptune had a dynamic atmosphere, with fast-moving clouds driven by winds of up to 400 miles per hour. A storm, the size of earth, raged continuously. Six new moons were added to the two already known about.

DNA Fingerprinting convicts criminal

THE FIRST TRIAL in Britain to be clinched by the new technique of DNA fingerprinting took place in April when Tony MacLean, the 'Notting Hill rapist', was convicted. The DNA pattern of the human cell is different for every individual, and by extracting DNA from blood, semen and other human fluids, scientists can now identify exactly who was present at the scene of a crime with a much greater degree of accuracy than was possible before. DNA can also be used to establish paternity beyond reasonable doubt.

Nuclear fusion flop

WHAT MIGHT HAVE BEEN the biggest scientific story of the year turned into a fiasco. It began in March when physicists at the University of Utah announced that they had achieved nuclear fusion in a test tube, using two special types of hydrogen, tritium and deuterium, obtainable from sea water. Fusion occurs when two nuclei of the lightest of all elements, hydrogen, fuse together to form one single, slightly-heavier atom, whose mass is less than the sum of the masses of the original nuclei. According to Einstein's famous equation, $E = mc^2$, the missing mass is converted into energy, without the radioactive waste left behind by nuclear fission, the basis of traditional nuclear power. It is fusion deep inside the sun that produces its heat, and scientists have long dreamt of achieving the same effect using cheap elements on Earth as a solution to all mankind's energy problems. The excitement generated by the Utah experiments did not last long, however. Neither the scientists there nor any elsewhere were able to repeat the experiment, and the dream of cheap, limitless, environmental-friendly energy went back to the drawing board.

Satellite TV gets off to a poor start

BRITAIN'S FIRST INDEPENDENT satellite television station, Rupert Murdoch's Sky TV, was launched in February. Although it promised to increase consumer choice, it proved to be a disappointing mixture of old sit-coms and overplayed movies – ammunition for those who had argued the independent TV channel would mean more but worse. Commercially it was a flop: few households had bought satellite dishes by the end of the year.

Time Chart

World News	Sport and the Arts	Science and Technology

1980

(February) Ayatollah Khomeini declares Holy War.
(April) Zimbabwe becomes independent.
Iranian Embassy siege in London.
(July) Brandt Report published.
(August) Strike at Lenin shipyard, Gdansk.
(September) Solidarity formed.
 Gulf War begins.
(November) Reagan elected in USA.

(April) *Dallas* reaches audience of 22 m in Britain.
(May) Nottingham Forest win European Cup.
(July) Borg wins 5th Wimbledon.
Moscow Olympics.
(December) John Lennon shot.

(March) UN report on world wildlife in danger.
(September) Pictures of Saturn from *Voyager 1*.

1981

(January) Hostages in Iran released.
SDP founded in Britain.
(April) Brixton riots.
(July) Toxteth riots.
Marriage of Prince of Wales.
(October) Assassination of Sadat.
(December) Martial law in Poland.
Women's peace camp set up at Greenham Common.

(March) First London marathon.
(July) McEnroe wins Wimbledon.
Memorable test match between England and
 Australia.
(August) MTV set up .
Coe and Ovett smash 1500 m records.

(April) First flight of space shuttle *Columbia*.
(September) French high-speed train begins
 service between Paris and Lyon.

1982

(April) Argentina invades Falklands.
(June) Argentinians surrender in Falklands.
Israel invades Lebanon.
(September) Massacre at Sabra and Shatila refugee
 camps.
(October) Employment Bill in Britain.
(November) Walesa released.

(July) Italy win World Cup.
(September) Daley Thompson sets new decathlon
 world record.
(October) *Mary Rose* raised.
(November) Channel 4 opens.

(November) Space shuttle launches its first
 satellite.
The Fate of the Earth published.
Compact discs on sale in Japan.
(December) Barney Clarke receives first
 artificial heart.

1983

(March) Reagan announces SDI.
(May) Tories win British general election.
(July) Martial law ended in Poland.
(August) Benigno Aquino assassinated in
 Philippines.
(September) Korean airliner shot down over USSR.
(October) US marines invade Grenada.

(January) Breakfast TV begins in Britain.
(April) Football League signs sponsorship deal with
 Cannon.

(January) Infra-red astronomy satellite
 launched.
Soviet satellite falls out of orbit.
(February) Drought causes bush fires in
 Australia.
(March) Scientists warn of greenhouse effect.
Barney Clarke dies.
(June) Sally Ride becomes first US woman in
 space.

1984

(March) Miners' strike begins in Britain.
(June) Indian army storms Golden Temple at
 Amritsar.
(September) Hong Kong agreement between Britain
 and China.
(October) News of Ethiopian famine reaches West.
Assassination of Mrs Gandhi.
Brighton bombing during Conservative Party
 Conference.
(November) Reagan re-elected in USA.

(February) Torvill and Dean break Olympic ice
 dance record.
(April) First cable TV channels open in Britain.
Zola Budd becomes British citizen.
(August) Los Angeles Olympics.
(December) Band Aid record released.

(April) AIDS virus identified.
(July) Warnock report.
(December) Bhopal disaster.

Time Chart

World News	Sport and the Arts	Science and Technology

1985

(February) Terry Waite negotiates freeing of hostages in Libya.
(March) Gorbachev takes over as leader in USSR. Miners' strike ends.
(June) TWA hijack. Air India plane blows up.
(July) State of emergency in South Africa.
(October) *Achille Lauro* hijack.
(November) Anglo-Irish agreement. Geneva summit.

(May) Heysal disaster.
(July) Live Aid concert. Becker becomes youngest player ever to win Wimbledon.
(August) Cram and Aouita break four world records between them.
(September) Pete Rose breaks 60-year-old baseball record.

(October) Rock Hudson dies of AIDS. Hole found in ozone layer.

1986

(January) Westland scandal.
(February) Marcos deposed in Philippines. Gorbachev introduces ideas of glasnost and perestroika.
(April) Chernobyl explosion. USA bombs Tripoli.
(August) Commonwealth leaders clash over South African sanctions.
(October) Reykjavik summit.
(November) Iran-Contra scandal breaks.
(December) Sakharov released.

(July) World Cup in Mexico.
(August) Chicago Bears play in London.
(November) *Spycatcher* court case opens in Australia.
Independent published.

(January) *Challenger* disaster. Channel Tunnel agreement signed.
(February) Halley's comet flies close to sun.
(August) William Schroeder second man to receive an artificial heart dies.

1987

(January) Waite disappears in Lebanon.
(March) *Herald of Free Enterprise* sinks off Zeebrugge.
(June) Tories win third election in a row.
(October) Stock market collapse.
(November) Enniskillen bombing.
(December) INF treaty signed.

(March) Van Gogh's 'Sunflowers' sell for record price.
(October) Tyson beats Biggs to become undisputed heavyweight champion of world.
(December) *Children of the Arbat* published in USSR and sells out within hours.
Gatting/Rana row during English cricket tour of Pakistan.

(February) Supernova found in Milky Way.
(September) Montreal Agreement signed.

1988

(February) Rioting breaks out between Armenia and Azerbaijan.
(April) Geneva agreement signed.
(June) Moscow summit.
(July) Ceasefire in Gulf.
(August) First Soviet troops withdraw from Afghanistan.
(November) Bush elected President of USA. Benazir Bhutto elected Prime Minister of Pakistan.
(December) Gorbachev's speech to UN on need to end Cold War.

(May) European football championships in West Germany.
(June) Mandela concert.
(September) Olympic Games in Seoul; Ben Johnson drug scandal.
(November) White Paper on future of British broadcasting.

(April) First foetal cell transplants as cure for Parkinson's disease.
(October) New US space shuttle, *Discovery*, takes off.
(November) Soviet shuttle *Burin* in orbit.
(December) Soviet cosmonauts land after record 370 days in orbit.

1989

(January) Seven-year ban on Solidarity lifted.
(June) Bloodshed in Tiananmen Square after students demonstrate for democracy. Green parties secure major successes in European elections.
(October) Walter Sisulu released. Guildford Four freed.
(November) The Berlin Wall opens.
(December) Civil War in Romania, and Ceausescu is sentenced to death.

(February) Salman Rushdie goes into hiding after death threat from the Ayatollah.
(April) Hillsborough Stadium disaster as Liverpool fans crushed to death.
(September) Europe retain the Ryder Cup.

(March) Nuclear fusion success, but not repeated.
(August) *Voyager 2* sends back pictures from Neptune.

Key figures of the decade

Mrs Corazon Aquino (b.1933)

WIDOW OF BENIGNO AQUINO, leading opponent of President Marcos of Philippines. Although without political experience, she stood against Marcos in the 1986 elections and won. Became President of Philippines after Marcos' flight into exile February 1986.

Benazir Bhutto (b.1953)

DAUGHTER of former Prime Minister Ali Zulfikar Bhutto of Pakistan, who was executed by the military government of General Zia in 1979. Long-time opponent of military rule there. In the elections held after death of President Zia in 1988, she became Pakistan's first civilian ruler for ten years and the first woman leader of a Muslim state.

George Bush (b.1924)

US AMBASSADOR to the United Nations 1970-3, US representative to China 1974-5 and Director of the CIA 1976. Chosen as Reagan's Vice-President 1980-8 and elected President in his own right in 1988.

Colonel Muammer Gadaffi (b.1942)

RULER OF LIBYA since 1969. Fervent supporter of Islamic causes and bitter enemy of the United States.

General Leopoldo Galtieri (b.1926)

HEAD OF MILITARY JUNTA that ruled Argentina 1977-83. President 1981-2. Man behind invasion of Falkland Islands in April 1982, which led to disastrous war with Britain. Ousted 1982. After Argentina's return to civilian rule in 1983, stood trial for human rights violations that took place under his rule and for incompetence during Falklands campaign. Acquitted on human rights charges in 1986 but given 12 years imprisonment for his role in the war.

Mrs Indira Gandhi (1917-84)

DAUGHTER OF JAWAHARLAL NEHRU, the first Prime Minister of independent India, who became a powerful political figure in her own right. Leader of Congress Party 1964-84 and Prime Minister of India 1966-77 and 1980-4. Assassinated by Sikhs in her own bodyguard after a serious outbreak of racial and religious tension in India in 1984. She was succeeded by her eldest son, Rajiv.

Bob Geldof (b.1954)

IRISH-BORN LEAD SINGER of the Boomtown Rats, who organized the Band Aid movement for famine relief in Ethiopia and inspired a whole string of similar efforts by pop stars and other celebrities in the mid 1980s.

Mikhail Gorbachev (b.1931)

SON OF PEASANT and Soviet Party official, who became the youngest Soviet leader since the war when he was chosen as Party Secretary in March 1985. Began a spectacular campaign of reform inside the USSR, which he called perestroika, and called for the end of the Cold War. The most remarkable Soviet leader in decades and a popular figure in the West.

General Wojciech Jaruzelski (b.1923)

POLISH ARMY OFFICER trained in the USSR and Prime Minister of Poland from February 1981. Brought in martial law in December 1981.

Ayatollah Ruhollah Khomeini (1900-89)

IRANIAN ISLAMIC religious leader, who became effective ruler of Iran after the downfall of the Shah in January 1979. Inspiration for Islamic revolution at home and crusade to spread fundamentalist Islam abroad. One of the great forces of the decade.

Neil Kinnock (b.1942)

LABOUR MP FOR ISLWYN (formerly Bedwellty) since 1970. Shadow Education Secretary 1979-82. Became leader of Labour Party in 1983. Belongs to the 'soft', non-Marxist left.

Key figures of the decade

Ferdinand Marcos (1917–89)

PRESIDENT AND VIRTUAL DICTATOR of Philippines since 1964. Ally of USA, who regarded him as a bulwark against the spread of communism in south-east Asia. Overthrown by popular revolution in aftermath of 1986 elections and went into exile in Hawaii.

Colonel Oliver North (b.1943)

MARINE OFFICER and Vietnam War hero who joined Reagan's National Security Council in 1981. Played a leading, if mysterious, role in the behind-the-scenes deals with Iran and the Nicaraguan Contras that became known as the Iran-Contra affair. Sacked in December 1986, he became – for a while – something of a hero among many Americans when he told Congress that he had acted out of patriotic motives and regretted nothing. By the time he came to trial in 1989, North was only indicted on minor charges like destroying official documents.

David Owen (b.1938)

DOCTOR who became Labour MP for Plymouth, Devonport in 1966. Foreign Secretary 1977-9. Broke with Labour Party in 1981 to become founder-member of SDP. Leader of SDP from 1983 and joint leader, with David Steel of the SDP-Liberal Alliance during 1987 election. Split with bulk of own party in 1987 over proposal to merge with Liberals. Now leader of a tiny group of SDP MPs in the Commons.

Ronald Reagan (b.1911)

REPUBLICAN. Governor of California 1966-74 and President of USA 1980-8. Became symbol of revival of US pride and confidence at home and abroad in 1980s.

Andrei Sakharov (1921–89)

LEADING SOVIET NUCLEAR PHYSICIST and dissident who became something of an international celebrity when he was condemned to exile in Gorky in 1980. Released by Gorbachev in 1986.

Arthur Scargill (b.1938)

LEFT-WING SOCIALIST and former member of British Communist Party who became President of National Union of Mineworkers in 1982 and led the struggle against pit closures that led to the 1984-5 strike. Regarded as something of a bogeyman by much of the British middle class.

Bruce Springsteen (b.1949)

AMERICAN ROCK SINGER, who sang of the troubles and joys of ordinary Americans, especially the young and working class. Two of his most popular albums were *Born to Run* (1975) and *Born in the USA* (1984), which sold 15 million copies world-wide and was adopted – quite mistakenly – by the Reagan administration as the anthem of American pride and patriotism.

Mrs Margaret Thatcher (b.1925)

MP FOR FINCHLEY since 1959, leader of the Conservative Party since 1975 and first woman Prime Minister of Britain since 1979. Re-elected with large majorities in 1983 and 1987 a twentieth-century record. A forceful personality, her contempt for socialism and vision of the 'enterprise culture' transformed Britain in the 1980s.

Terry Waite (b.1939)

SPECIAL ENVOY of the Archbishop of Canterbury, who won the respect of Colonel Gadaffi of Libya and was able to arrange the release of British hostages there. Took up cause of Western hostages in Lebanon and disappeared there in January 1987, presumed kidnapped.

Lech Walesa (b.1943)

ELECTRICIAN at the Lenin shipyard in Gdansk, Poland, who took a leading role in the 1980 strikes and the creation of the free trade union Solidarity. Became a symbol of Polish defiance against Communist dictatorship. Interned under martial law, December 1981 to November 1982. Remained active in Polish resistence throughout 1980s.

Books for further reading

It is too early for many books *about* the 1980s to have been published but below is a list of books, fiction and non-fiction, that helped to shape or describe the decade:

Books about the 1980s

Fiction

Tom Wolfe, *Bonfire of the Vanities*, Jonathan Cape, 1988 – a novel that paints a picture of New York in the 1980s

David Lodge, *Nice Work*, Secker and Warburg, 1988 – a comic novel set in the Britain of the early 1980s

Non-fiction

Ian Jack, *Before the Oil ran out; Britain 1977-86*, Fontana, 1988

Terry Coleman, *Thatcher's Land*, Corgi, 1988

Gore Vidal, *Armageddon*, Andre Deutsch, 1987 – a satirical look at Reagan's USA

Martin Walker, *The Waking Giant*, Sphere, 1987 – the USSR in the 1980s by the *Guardian* correspondent there

M. Fathers and A. Higgins, *Tiananmen: The Rape of Peking*, Doubleday, 1989

Books that made a stir

Salman Rushdie, *The Satanic Verses*, Viking, 1988

Peter Wright, *Spycatcher*, Collins, 1988

Jonathan Schell, *The Fate of the Earth*, Cape, 1982

Stephen Hawking, *A Brief History of Time*, Bantam, 1988 – the book that made the new discoveries in astronomy accessible to the ordinary reader

J. Elkington and J. Hailes, *The Green Consumer's Supermarket Shopping Guide*, Gollancz, 1989

Brian Gould, *A Future for Socialism*, Cape 1989 – how the Labour Party should adapt to the new middle class Britain

Acknowledgments

Allsport/Steve Powell for pages 31, 58 and 64; Associated Press Ltd for page 5; Camera Press for pages 10, 14, 15, 16, 22, 34, 42, 51, 54, 57, 61 and 64; Fotokhronika Tass for page 38; Gamma/Frank Spooner for pages 30, 36, 37, 41, 45, 60, 62 and 65; Hulton-Deutsch Collection for pages 4, 6 and 27; Keystone Collection for pages 3,9, 13, 18 and 20; Magnum for page 26; NASA for pages 16 and 47; National Film Archive for pages 22 and 58; Popperfoto for pages 24, 32, 40, 44, 50 and 52; Rex Features for page 56; Sipa Press for page 48.

Index

Index